THE STORY OF THE DANCE

THE DANCE

the story of the dance told in pictures and text

by **JOHN MARTIN**

dance critic of The New York Times

TUDOR PUBLISHING COMPANY · NEW YORK

CONTENTS

PART ONE

Basic dance

DANCING is a very broad term, since it includes a multiplicity of activities ranging all the way from certain natural and instinctive practices of animals, birds and fish to the most elaborate and carefully planned artistic creations of especially gifted men and women. It is all dancing, however, and in spite of many variations in outward appearance and inward motivation, it is all basically the same thing.

This essential unity makes what might seem to be a complex subject actually a very simple one. Once we have grasped the key to its structure we can open at will all of its doors and follow any of its numerous corridors as far as our interest dictates. Sometimes one or another of us without the master key may stumble into a particular corridor by a back entrance, and lacking any awareness of the edifice as a whole, take for granted that this single corridor is all there is to the building. Thus we may find the anthropologist so completely concerned with ceremonial dances of savage tribes that he ignores the ballet as mere idle amusement; or the ballet enthusiast, perhaps, looking down on the folk dance as crude and obsolete; or both of them possibly frowning on the "jitterbug" as an undisciplined vulgarian.

But as a matter of fact, the most sacred ritual dance of a primitive people, the French court ballet and the Lindy Hop are all simply different aspects, different stages of development, of exactly the same thing; at their roots, if we trace them back, we will find them to be quite indis-

Hoop Dance as performed at the annual Inter-Tribal Ceremonial, Gallup, New Mexico.

6

tinguishable from each other. They are all outgrowths of what might be called basic dance, which is the same in all parts of the world, in all times and cultures. It is, indeed, a fundamental element of man's behavior. When we have understood what basic dance is, therefore, we shall have got hold of the master key.

To understand it is simplicity itself. Nature has so constituted us that movement is the medium in which we live our lives, not only in our internal physiological mechanisms but in our outward conduct. It is by means of movement that we dress ourselves, prepare and eat our breakfast, board the bus for work and carry on our business, whether it happens to be digging ditches or adding columns of figures. Much of this movement is so habitual that we

Blackfoot ceremony danced by Grant Code as a concert number. Franziska Boas, drummer.

Reginald Laubin in an authentic Cheyenne Brave Heart Dance.

La Argentina in a gypsy dance from the Spanish ballet, "Sonatina," 1928.

are scarcely aware of it. The rest of it is generally rational and orderly; that is, we see something to be done and take the logical steps to do it. To this end we are equipped with an elaborate nervous system whose sole business it is to carry the reports of our senses about the objects and conditions around us to the proper set of muscles so that suitable action can be taken with regard to those objects and conditions.

Sometimes, however, these processes do not seem to operate in so orderly a manner. For example, when a terrific noise occurs unex-

Mexican folk dance from the revue, "Mexicana," sponsored by the Mexican Government.

Argentinita in a classic Spanish dance.

pectedly close behind us, we "jump out of our skins," as the saying goes; that is, we make a combination of violent and totally irrelevant movements, probably grabbing our heads or throwing our arms into the air. Or at another time we hear enormously good news, and "jump for joy," hugging ourselves and skipping about the room in movements that, once again, have no bearing whatever on the news we have received. Or still another time, we are deeply agitated with worry and, with hands clutching each other, heads bent and faces scowling, we "walk the floor"—which really gets us nowhere in a practical sense.

Why do we do these things? Because we are in a stirred-up emotional state; our nervous systems are charging our muscles with impulses to move and we cannot rationalize about what movements to make. Like a flood breaking through a dam, these motor impulses break through without waiting for planned direction. But it is important to note that the movements we make under these circumstances have a certain consistency about them in spite of being irrational, and they are by no means unrelated to the emotional states that prompt them. For example, when we are worried we do not skip about the room hugging ourselves, and when we are startled by a sudden noise we do not walk the floor. The movements themselves actually have in them the essential nature of the emotional experience, even though we have not rationally directed them and they do not specifically "mean" anything.

It follows, then, that any emotional state tends to express itself in movements which may not be practically useful or in any way representational, but nevertheless reflect the specific character and

Juan and Soledad Martinez.  Carmen Amaya, Spanish gypsy dancer.

quality of that emotional state. Working on this principle, consciously or unconsciously, all kinds of dancers have evolved all kinds of emotional dances. Religious dancers, carried away with the mystery of the unknown, dance themselves into a frenzy after the manner of the "holy rollers," the "holy jumpers," the Shakers, the whirling dervishes; high-spirited young men and women, excitedly aware of the attraction between the sexes, move gaily together in the measures of the ballroom dance; a sensitive artist, becoming emotionally aware of the splendor of a sunset, or of the nobility of a hero, or of the tragedy of the underprivileged, allows each of these impulses to express itself in movements which he deliberately remembers and develops in order to be able to convey to others something of his own intuitive reaction which is too deep for words.

Thus, at the root of all these varied manifestations of dancing (and of countless other manifestations, as well) lies the common impulse to resort to movement to externalize emotional states which we cannot externalize by rational means. This is basic dance.

Opposite: Rosario and Antonio, photographed in action by Gjon Mili.

VARIATIONS IN FORM

But though it is a universal urge, there is no such thing as a universal form in which it manifests itself, for the occasions which inspire it and the traditions which limit it vary over the face of the earth and throughout the course of history. This is not at all extraordinary, as becomes apparent if we compare it with another biological drive such as hunger. Eating is assuredly a universal practice, yet its forms differ immeasurably. Certain climates and soils produce only certain foods; dwellers along the sea are likely to make fish their major item of diet while those in the wilderness eat game; various religions pronounce certain animals sacred or unclean and not to be eaten in either case; the growth of civilization substitutes cooked foods for raw ones, develops scientific methods of producing new foods, and leads in general to refinements of taste and even to elaborately complicated recipes to tempt the epicurean.

Exactly the same kinds of controlling influence color the styles and types of movement by which the universal biological motor drives are satisfied. Geography, climate, race, religion, social environment, physique, dress, cultural tradition, historical background, and the very passage of time itself, all affect the ways men move and, more particularly, the ways they translate movement into dance. Through a combination of all these causes we find the dances of the Orient confined in the main to small, slow movements, chiefly of the hands and upper body, with supple fingers bending backwards, toes turned upwards, and lateral movements of the head and neck that are virtually impossible to the western body; we find the African dancer centering his motion largely in the pelvic region, while the European ballet dancer maintains a rigid spine and departs from his Oriental brothers by extend-

Uday Shan-kar and his company in a classical Hindu dance-drama.

'Asadata Dafora in a traditional African dance.

Uday Shan-kar and his company in a dance-drama of modern India.

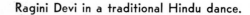
Ragini Devi in a traditional Hindu dance.

ing his toes sharply downwards; we find the Spanish dancer stamping vigorously on the ground while the ballet dancer touches it so lightly as to deny gravity.

All these systems have undergone extensive changes within themselves as history has developed around them. Primitive ceremonials, originally vital and inspired, have been perpetuated from generation to generation until the vitality and inspiration have passed completely out of them and not even the chieftains and high priests can remember their links to experience, understand the words that accompany them or supply any significance to the empty shell of movements that has survived. In the early period of the European court ballet the dancers impersonated gods of the Greek and Roman mythology, for in the Renaissance society of the time there was a strong desire to pattern behavior upon the graciousness and dignity that classic antiquity seemed to them to contain and contemporary custom to lack. Later when the revival of Gothic mysticism swept over European culture in the early nineteenth century and the Middle Ages seemed to hold the secret of a much-desired spiritual re-awakening, the ballet turned to supernatural matters and all the dancers assumed characterizations of haunted maidens risen from the tomb, or became mythical creatures who inhabited the air and spurned what was earthly and mortal.

Evelyne and Beatrice Kraft, American dancers of Hindu dance, who have popularized it in revues, night clubs and moving pictures.

Left: Hadassah in a Javanese court dance, "Golek." Right: Raden Mas Wiradat, a leading dancer in Soerakarta, Java.

16

Hadassah in her comedy adaptation of Hindu dancing called "Broadway Hindu."

It is impossible to say that any of these approaches is exclusively right or wrong, better or worse than any other; they all arose out of an inner need and completely satisfied that need—just as we "jump out of our skins" when we are suddenly frightened or hug ourselves when we are overjoyed. They are all absolutely right, therefore, for the specific circumstances under which they have been created.

For us to enjoy them fully as spectators it is incumbent upon us to approach them in this way, not finding fault with the ballet because it does not beat its heels into the ground, or with the Hindu dance because it does not leap and whirl, or with the so-called modern dance because it does not rise upon the points of its toes. When we relate any form of dance to the inward motivations which are responsible for its form, we open the door to its full enjoyment. Naturally, the dance which grows out of motivations common to our own time and society will have the greatest appeal for us, since its motivations belong specifically to us. If other forms are inevitably exotic and consequently inspire a more objective response in us, they are by no means dull or incomprehensible on that account.

BASIC MUSIC

Thus far movement has been the sole subject under consideration, for movement is the fundamental stuff of dancing. Nevertheless, only in a comparatively small section of the world and in comparatively modern times are dance and music separable arts. In Europe and America, while we rarely find dancing without music, we have a large musical art quite independent of dancing. In by far the greater part of the world, however, such a concept is altogether alien; music without dancing and dancing without music are equally unlikely.

As a matter of fact, the relationship between movement and music is not merely a matter of custom but is a basic relationship. To revert once again to our earlier illustrations, when we are frightened by a sudden noise we do not react silently; in addition to our startled movements we almost invariably emit some kind of cry. Similarly, when we skip jubilantly about, in all probability we make some sort of "joyful noise." When all the body is activated by some strong emotion, there is no reason to expect the voice to remain silent.

La Meri, American ethnological dancer in (left) a Burmese Pwe; (right) a Hindu dance, "Deva Murti."

La Meri in Javanese "Slendang."

La Meri in (top) an Arabian café dance, "Chethat-al-Maharma"; (bottom) the Philippine dance-game, "Tinikling."

Huapala in a Hawaiian hula.

In his beginnings the dancer inevitably sings as he dances. When, however, his movements become too strenuous and demand too much breath for him to continue his song, the bystanders take up the singing for him. In time the melodic line of the voice is transferred to an instrument, and since it can play higher and lower than he could possibly sing, it serves even to increase his range of expression. Similarly, the rhythmic beating of his feet on the ground is accentuated, and intensified beyond what he could do himself, by the clapping of hands, the shaking of rattles and the beating of drums. Eventually the accompanying song may be extended until it is played by a whole symphony orchestra, but if it is really dance music it still retains the rhythmic pulse of his body and the melodic line of his voice; it is still, indeed, potentially the dancer's own song.

Both in movement and in music, from time to time, certain practices which were orginally spontaneous and alive become stereotyped and mechanical through mere surface repetition. The dancers

Sai Shoki in a Korean dance.

Huapala in a Hawaiian hula showing the influence of the white missionaries and the "Mother Hubbard" dress.

look backward at tradition instead of inward at creation; the musicians forget their function of voicing the dancer's song and instead merely put together sounds for their own sakes. Then the history of dancing, and of music, records a low period. But since dancing is at bottom a biological function, it must necessarily renew itself. In every barren period, accordingly, rebels arise who break through the intrenched traditionalism and set up fresh currents to replace it.

No form is permanent, definitive, ultimate; only the basic principle of dance is enduring, and out of it, like the cycle of nature itself, rises an endless succession of new springs out of old winters.

Left: Tei Ko in a concert version of a classic Chinese dance. Right: Kikugoro the Sixth, master dancer-actor of Japan.

PART TWO

Dance for the sake of the dancer

DANCING falls naturally into two major categories: that that is done for the emotional release of the individual dancers, without regard to the possible interest of a spectator; and that, on the other hand, that is done for the enjoyment of the spectator either as an exhibition of skill, the telling of a story, the presentation of pleasurable designs, or the communication of emotional experience. The second category is largely an outgrowth of the first, but both play important parts in the picture as a whole.

In primitive societies, in which there is no knowledge of natural laws by which seeds grow and crops ripen, animals and humans bear young, or sickness is healed, every manifestation of these commonplaces of life becomes a separate hazard, the outcome of which is unpredictable. Fears easily arise that perhaps this time the seed will refuse to sprout and there will be no grain to harvest, that the sun will not shine or the rain consent to fall. With no awareness of the orderly principles of nature, such an overwrought state of emotion is not to be assuaged by reason, but only by venting itself in movement. When, as a matter of fact, the grain does ripen, the sun does shine and the rain fall, these dances assume in the primitive mind the position of causative forces and are established as ritual.

Every important event of tribal life is accompanied by suitable dances, for they are all mystical experiences; birth, the arrival of the youth at manhood, marriage, the stalking of game, the conquest of enemies, death and the assurance that the dead will remain in the grave instead of returning to make trouble, the appeasing of evil spirits who in time past have brought specific disaster, and the honoring (or perhaps more accurately the bribing) of beneficent spirits who have bestowed blessings, all inspire emotional uncertainties which must be somehow resolved.

In some cases, these dances of high emotional tension consist of rather hysterical random movements and lead to frenzy, catalepsy and trance; but in the vast majority of instances, their magic is of a more consistent, and, indeed, a more demonstrable character. If, for example, one wishes the corn to grow tall, one suggests it and practically demands it by leaping high, over and over, in the presence of the corn. If the deer is to be hunted, one dons antlers and bits of fur and performs in advance with meticulous accuracy the conduct expected of the quarry from the earliest moment of the chase to the death struggle. By similar processes of pre-enactment, beneficial results are produced upon friends and destructive results upon enemies; and the more exact the mimicry the more certain the efficaciousness of the ritual.

Such magic is not only characterized by appropriateness in every case, but is also based on a logical premise which we in more sophisticated societies are far too prone to ignore. This premise is the inherent contagion that exists in bodily movement. We are so constituted that we yawn when others yawn, laugh when they laugh, weep when they weep, feel sympathetic muscular strains when we watch others struggling under heavy loads, and are stimulated to dance when they dance. When we see a body undergoing muscular exertion, we are naturally inclined to feel it reflected in our own musculatures.

In primitive societies spectators watching a dancer are frequently drawn first into beating a drum for him and then into actually dancing in the ring with him, executing the same steps that he is executing. If this kind of persuasiveness has been experienced in one's own self, why should one not expect it to be experienced as a matter of course by the deer that is to be hunted, the enemy that is to be destroyed, the corn in the ground? To simple peoples, this power of dance to persuade others to imitate it seems supernatural and is employed accordingly; to us it is a scientifically established psychological process, and it constitutes the basis on which we enjoy watching the dance and on which we understand the emotional experience that the dancer is trying to communicate to us.

These primitive imitative dances are not originally planned to be watched by spectators, but only to control the actions of animals, spirits, gods and enemies, who are most probably not even present.

Haitian ritual dance, "Yanvalou-Jenou."

Inevitably, however, the particular excellence of some dancer as a mimic must win the especial admiration of the bystanders, and sooner or later we find the development of mimetic dancing for its own sake with only secondary accent upon magic and religion. Out of this root there emerges eventually the quite separate art of the drama, with the music of the dancer's song replaced by the spoken words which are suitable to the character he is imitating. Ultimately not only magic and religion, but also dance movement itself, have passed out of the picture and the purely literary drama has come into being.

FOLK DANCING

The "magic" powers of dancing have at least one other important manifestation that must be noted. When the men of a tribe perform a war dance, it is not exclusively for its mimetic influence over the enemy; it is also for the establishment of solidarity in the tribe itself. It is a fact that when an individual dances in unison with a great number of other individuals, he has a sense of participating in a mass movement far greater than anything he could possibly do alone. The group becomes one in conscious strength and purpose, and each individual experiences a heightened power as part of it. Such a principle underlies the military parade, in which the object is to establish the individual marcher (and the onlooker, as well, who participates in a sense through the contagion of movement) as part of a unity infinitely more powerful than himself. When a mile of marching men steps forward on its collective right foot, it is a tremendous step for all to participate in!

This feeling of oneness with one's fellows which is established by collective dancing is one of the principal reasons for the growth and persistence of folk dancing, whether in the olden days or at this very moment. Most of the ritual dances that we have been dealing with are really dancing by the folk, but it is customary to group them in a class of their own, and to consider folk dancing as chiefly recreational in intent. To be sure, harvest celebrations and other common occasions for folk celebration still retain something of their original ritual significance, such as thanksgiving to divine powers, offerings to assure good crops, symbolic rites to bless a marriage with many sons, and the like; but these aspects have a way of fading into the remote background and leaving the element of simple and hearty play in the ascendancy.

Man is a gregarious animal, and by his very nature has to assemble with his kind every so often and rejoice in the kinship. In the days when travel was difficult and distances were long, it was a matter almost of survival for the people of the countryside to hitch up their teams and meet at some fairly central spot for a long and energetic session of dancing once in a while. In no other way could they remind themselves that they were members of a single community, with common interests and tastes and habits; and having contributed something of physical and emotional vigor to the common activity, each one returned to his isolated home with a larger share of the community strength than he had given.

If people wonder why folk dancing has grown nowadays to even larger dimensions than it en-

Opposite: Couple from an American square set.

Left: Swedish Ox Dance for two men. Right: Swedish folk dance for one man and two girls.

joyed in those simpler and less congested days and has been embraced enthusiastically by city dwellers, the reason is exactly the same. The city dweller, though he lives so close to his neighbors in a physical sense that there is scarcely elbow room, has just as little genuine contact with them as the isolated peasant. There must accordingly be frequent occasions arranged when he can quit battling with his anonymous fellows for a seat on the subway and buffeting them about in the frantic processes of business, in order to assemble with them on purely social grounds and reestablish their common interests and fundamental fellowship as human beings. Community dancing does not deal in personal differences, bargaining or argument; it is on a far more universal and elementary level than that. It simply affirms the underlying emotional oneness of all men, and sends each of them home reinvigorated with the strength of the common heritage of the race. This is the truly social basis of the dance.

THE CYCLE OF BALLROOM DANCING

The folk dancing that is so popular with us today has undergone many refinements, to be sure, since the Middle Ages when, roughly speaking, its present forms began to take shape. In its beginnings it was the lusty and uninhibited emotional expression of crude and unpolished peoples. Its

Left: Polish Oberek. Right: Ukrainian Kolomeyka.

attitude toward sex was likely to be altogether frank, and the many varieties of couple dances that evolved were openly designed for purposes of courtship. Why else, indeed, should a man and woman dance together? But if these were honest and healthy dances, they were not notable for reticence or refinement.

This was the general status and character of the dancing of the simple people of Europe at the dawn of the Renaissance, and it constituted something of a problem. Obviously, rude and unmannerly peasant practices, however true to nature and to the needs of emotional release, could not be allowed in the ballrooms of the new aristocracy, yet the new aristocracy could not be expected to forego dancing, for it had exactly the same impulses as the peasants.

Before we can fully understand the important effects of this situation upon the future of both the social and the art dance, it is necessary to consider briefly who this new aristocracy was. The princes of the Italian Renaissance were neither nobly born nor nobly bred. As a class they were men without background, culture or scruples. Many of them were condottieri; that is, mercenary soldiers or in many instances virtually gangsters, who sold their allegiance to the highest bidder. Their titles were sometimes bought, sometimes stolen and sometimes taken by the sword. They were unfitted for leadership in every respect except material power and a curious ambition which was partly personal and partly (if only subconsciously) concerned with the amelioration of the race of men.

This ambition is perhaps the salient aspect of the Renaissance. Throughout the Middle Ages men had been taught to think of themselves as poor wretches without individual worth, as sinners who, unless they made fantastic atonement throughout their earthly lives, could look forward only to an eternity in the fires of hell. Life was physically hard, mentally fearful, dominated by superstition, and without hope. It is not difficult to understand why at length in the fourteenth century, after a succession of world catastrophes, wars, plagues, fires, the general state of the human mind was so disturbed that it had to seek outlet for its pent-up emotional conditions in such irrational mass manifestations as the dance manias. Whole communities of people then were stricken with a kind of madness that sent them dancing and gyrating through the streets and from village to village for days at a time until they died in agonized exhaustion.

Out of the same emotional causes grew that bitter and terrible art form, the Dance of Death. This was a kind of dramatic ceremonial whose scene was the graveyard. In it Death called upon each stratum of society—a king, a pope, a soldier, a peasant, a mother, a child, and so forth—and led them all at last in a grim processional into the tomb. This was in effect a desperate statement of the common man's disillusionment with the entire social, political and religious scheme under which he lived; Death leveled all ranks and stations and proved them all ultimately vain.

It is obvious from our present perspective on the scene that these outbursts were indications of the crumbling of the medieval basis of thought. A great emotional rebellion was expressing itself; not rationally, because it did not know intellectually where to turn, but in that inevitable first medium for venting pent-up emotional states, movement and its more formal manifestation, dance.

If such phenomena as these were chiefly negative, indicating the collapse of the medieval system rather than the erection of any new systems, they led directly into the more positive aspect of the situation which we have come to call the Renaissance. This was literally a rebirth. Men threw off the old concept of themselves as wretched slaves to mysticism and declared themselves to be emancipated, self-acting individuals. They probably had very little idea what to do with this newly discovered freedom of thought and conduct, but at this revolutionary juncture an unrelated event in a distant part of the world served to shape their direction and progress. In the middle of the fifteenth century the Ottoman Turks captured Constantinople. Here for centuries in this eastern capital of the Roman Empire had been preserved the classic culture of Greece and Rome, which had been undermined and largely destroyed in Rome itself when the barbarians from the north had invaded that western capital of the empire. Now, with the fall of Constantinople, the scholars fled once more to the west, and brought back with them the carefully nurtured scholarship, the artistic lore and the tradition of the ancient culture. It was rich, elegant and pagan, and it offered to the searching minds of the time exactly the kind of model they needed in order to build a new system of life for themselves entirely contrary to the old one against which they were rebelling.

To be sure, this classic revival affected chiefly the wealthy courtiers, for the common man—still poor, still illiterate, still ill-used—had little contact with refinements of culture. What got to him, seeped down from the top. But it was something. Festivals in honor of the Christian saints were re-dedicated to the gods of Olympus, and all the practices of medieval life were reoriented to follow the pagan precedent of the ancient practices, or rather to follow the current ideas—sometimes rather fantastic and generally quite inaccurate, in spite of the scholars from Constantinople—of what those practices had been.

What was of paramount importance, however, was that man had emerged in his own eyes as a creature of inherent dignity, with the capacity to make his life what he wanted it to be. But the contrast between this ideal and what he actually saw of himself was rather marked; he was still a crude, mannerless lout, who ate like an animal, walked like a clodhopper, and generally comported himself like a peasant. For the princes of the day with their regal palaces, their silk and satin raiment, their pretensions to leadership, this was an impossible situation. Scholars and tutors were attached to the individual courts to remedy intellectual shortcomings, but of equal importance were the dancing masters who were brought in to remedy the gross defects of carriage and deportment. It was the duty of these gentlemen to teach their masters and mistresses how to manipulate their heavy and voluminous costumes—the men their long shoes stretching out so far in front that the tips had to be fastened to the knees in order to make walking possible, their swords which bade fair to trip them at every step; the ladies their ruffs and headdresses and yards of train. Clearly the old dances of the countryside were now both impracticable and utterly unsuitable in manner and style; it was up to the dancing masters to create new and more suitable ones.

And here ballroom dancing was born.

By all this the common people were blissfully unaffected; they continued to dance as they had always done. What is more, the dancing masters took as the basis for the elegant routines they

A weekly session of the Community Folk Dance Center, directed by Michael Herman, photographed in action at Arlington Hall, New York.

evolved for the courtiers these very dances of the common people, refined them, toned them down and made them intricate and complicated. In fact, so void of spontaneity and spirit did they ultimately become—so lacking in the elements of basic dance—that courtiers frequently slipped away quietly and joined the dances of the much despised common people, where they could really find some outlet for their emotional exuberance. This practice became so general, indeed, that Castiglione, who was more or less the Emily Post of the early sixteenth century, wrote in effect that it was quite all right socially to join these vulgar revels so long as a mask was worn to indicate that the courtier was aware that he was "slumming."

Yet manifestly the formal dances of the dancing masters would not have survived and developed as they did if they had been totally barren of emotional satisfaction. It was a special emotion, a new one born of the new direction of life, that they were created to satisfy, and obviously did satisfy—the passionate desire for personal elegance and social authority.

Throughout all the five hundred years of its history to date, the ballroom dance has continued to be torn between these two extremes. On the one hand, polite society requires that it be well-mannered, strictly ordered in form, gracious—and unemotional; on the other hand, human nature demands that it serve as a free and unhampered release for emotions, and in couple dances that it make no false pretenses about sex. It is nature, of course, that produces the creative dances, and no matter how much polite society frowns upon them, it inevitably has to admit them into its sedate ballrooms sooner or later, making what modifications it can force upon them, but always having to swallow a good deal of its own prudishness.

From the days of the Renaissance right down to today, every dance that has won popularity in conservative circles has had its origins among the "vulgar." The minuet, probably the most mincing and refined of all court dances at its height, began life as a bouncing couple dance of the peasants. The waltz, which was a rambunctious whirling dance centuries ago in Germany, shocked the better people of the nineteenth century ballroom to the core by daring to allow dancers to stand face to face in each other's arms. Now it is held up as a prime example of old-fashioned modesty by that older generation which finds jazz dancing revoltingly coarse. The turkey trot of 1910 marched straight out of the underworld, but its freedom of movement was so convincing that society overcame its first horror and embraced it warmly. The beginnings of the tango and the rumba and the Lindy are much the same, and each of them has had to face the opprobrium of the conservative before it has finally won admission to well-bred ballrooms. Now even the jitterbug, only recently scorned and denounced, has been pronounced acceptable by the official dancing masters—with a few modifications, of course.

It is a cycle that must inevitably continue, for recreational dancing, done solely for the sake of providing the dancer with a release for his inner compulsions, no longer serves its purpose when that release is denied. No matter how pretty a dance may be to watch, unless it gives something to the dancer, it is doomed. The couple dance is forever and exclusively a courtship dance; for the satisfaction of other social emotions, the square and circle and longways dances of folk origin have once again found themselves in demand, and by the urban sophisticates. Between them they present a broad and healthy program for the contemporary ballroom, and in spite of adaptations and compromises, still maintain identifiable relationships to basic dance.

PART THREE

Dance as Spectacle

IT IS easy to understand how the tendencies of the Renaissance courts made the outward appearance of the dance of more importance than its inward satisfactions, or rather how the inward satisfactions now came to depend largely on the perfection of the outward appearance. Some of the instructions of the most famous masters of the time which still survive lay emphasis upon the necessity of pleasing the eye of the bystander. And this transformation of the essential character of the dance from a mere type of play to a vehicle for the display of personal skills and graces is one of the major sources of the development of that form of dance art that came to be known as the ballet.

Needless to say, it was not the only source; nor was this the earliest manifestation, by any means, of dancing designed primarily to please the spectator. In primitive cultures, as well as in the highly developed cultures of Greece and Rome, it was a common practice for slaves to perform for the entertainment of their masters. There is no evidence that this was dancing of a very high order, though in the days of the later Roman emperors, it is true, there grew up a type of performer known as the pantomimus who, in spite of his characteristic decadence, may well have been an artist of considerable attainments in many instances. It is inaccurate, of course, to class the great choric theatre of ancient Greece as spectacle, for the thousands of spectators who attended the annual performances did so as participants in a religious rite and not as pleasure-seekers.

After the fall of Rome, jugglers, tumblers, mountebanks wandered widely over the land, now attaching themselves to the household of some wealthy lord, now playing at fairs and in city streets. Among them dancing was definitely practiced, though again not on a very high level. Such roving dancers and acrobats existed all through the Middle Ages; and later in the Renaissance, still attached to the households of the various lords, they made signal contributions as professionals to the advancement of the spectacular dance as it grew up in the courts.

Out of the teeming life of the Middle Ages came many other influences to contribute ultimately to the ballet's form: processions, maskings and mummings, all of religious origin and many of them pre-Christian; tournaments which had grown into elaborately costumed spectacles of almost theatrical character; banquets in the great houses of the nobles during which floats representing

33

castles, ships, or even great pastries, were borne into the hall carrying companies of singers and dancers to entertain the diners and sometimes to induce them by dramatic presentations of battles between Christians and Saracens to participate in one of the crusades.

Here, indeed, was a rich and gorgeous mass of material to draw upon, but it was so conglomerate and diffuse that it might never have achieved any semblance of conscious artistry without the particular guidance of Renaissance thinking and the fundamental emotional drive that controlled that thinking. The revival of classical scholarship had brought to light the existence of the theatre of the ancient Greeks with its unity of music, poetry and dance, and such a vision served to inspire the musicians and the poets and the dancers to work toward a similar unity in the arts of their own time. Their specific knowledge of the Greek theatre was meager and largely inaccurate, but a mere glimpse of its underlying principles was enough to arouse their enthusiasm. In France shortly after the middle of the sixteenth century, musicians and poets banded together for this purpose in an Academy of Music and Poesy with a charter from the king; in Italy shortly afterwards a similar group was formed under the name of the Camerata. The former actually accomplished nothing, but out of the latter's efforts emerged the early form of opera.

THE COURT BALLET

Exactly this same impulse toward reviving the unity of the Greek theatre gave the world what was really its first ballet. It came about in the French court at the instigation of the queen-mother, Catherine de' Medici. She was the daughter of one of the greatest houses in Italy, where progress in the dance, music and all the other arts was far ahead of anything the French had accomplished. When she had come to France as the queen of Henry II, therefore, she had brought with her a company of musicians and dancers from her native city to supervise her artistic presentations, and highly impressive these were.

But the "Ballet Comique de la Reine," produced in 1581, outdid them all. Catherine herself was not primarily interested in its artistry, but for political reasons she wanted to offer something of unprecedented splendor, and took as a suitable occasion the wedding of the sister of the queen, her daughter-in-law. The important commission of producing such a work fell to her valet de chambre, chief violinist and dancing master, Balthasar de Beaujoyeaux, who, in spite of the French form he had given his name, was an Italian. Beaujoyeaux, stirred by the same ambitions as his colleagues to restore the concept of the ancient Greeks, embraced this as his great opportunity. The poetry he commissioned to be written by one of the court poets, the instrumental music by one of the court musicians and the vocal music by another (for at that time the same composer rarely wrote for both voice and instruments). He himself devised the dances and supervised the spectacle. Its story, which seems dull and inconsequential to us, dealt with a Greek hero who was enchanted by Circe and at last freed by the intervention of the gods; but what was important about it was that for the first time a court spectacle of this sort confined itself to a consistent dramatic subject throughout, and all its verses, music and dancing were appropriate to the development of the theme.

The success of the experiment was complete. Thousands of common people attempted to obtain admission to the palace to see it, many of them having come from long distances. Copies of the work were printed and sent to all the courts of Europe, and Catherine's political ambitions were achieved as well as Beaujoyeaux's artistic ones. The court was virtually bankrupted by the production, however, as it had cost some 400,000 crowns. The artistic principles it introduced were practiced thereafter on a far more modest scale, if at all, but it had succeeded in establishing them as principles, and the seed it thus sowed was destined to bear fruit for many generations.

From this time on, the French court was the center of the ballet's development. Italy, its original home, had turned with greater interest to opera, a similar attempt at reviving the Greek unity of the arts but with its chief emphasis on music. Both this development and Italy's continued interest in elaborate scenic investiture and mechanical innovation were to exert strong influences on the ballet, but the form itself, in which the dance occupied the chief place in the artistic unity, was to continue for three hundred years as a predominantly French enterprise.

The court ballets which followed the "Ballet Comique" fell just as short of it in artistry as they did in costliness. Their actual forms varied in detail according to the individual tastes of the monarchs or the courtiers directly in charge, but in the main they consisted of a succession of dances (sometimes

Salome's dance before Herod as a medieval English artist conceived it, basing his opinion on the kind of dancing popular in his day.

The "Ballet Comique de la Reine" as pictured in the printed version of the work sponsored by Catherine de' Medici.

as many as thirty, rarely less than ten or twelve) by different groups of dancers representing related phases of some common subject. For example, a ballet (if it were a very small one) might consist of entrées representing Europe, Asia, Africa and America, with the participants in each entrée sumptuously clad in a style which, with its plumed headdresses, jewels, panniers and deeply skirted coats, only remotely suggested the natives of one of these quarters of the globe. The whole was brought to a conclusion by general dancing in which the entire court, duly masked, participated along with the dancers from the spectacle. The emphasis remained social, and the performers, except for a few extremely necessary professionals attached to the court, were amateurs.

Even the "Ballet Comique" itself with all its artistic innovations had not altered the essential pattern of the Renaissance ballroom in any great degree, either socially or physically. As at any court ball, the king and his household sat at the head of the room on a dais; along the sides of the hall, seated in the long galleries or standing along the edges of the floor itself, were the other spectators. At the far end of the hall was a shallow platform which served merely to house the representation of Circe's palace and was not a stage in any sense. The action all took place on the floor, with the audience on three sides of it. Such an overall plan, in spite of many internal changes of more or less importance, was to prevail for still the greater part of another century, until, indeed, the ballet itself declined as a court function and took other forms.

The intervening decades before this decline, however, saw an ever increasing delight in its practice by the court. When Louis XIII was king, a single performance in an evening was frequently not enough, and His Majesty and fellow dancers trouped from the royal palace to lesser houses giving a repetition in each, and bringing the night to a close with still another repetition on a great platform erected for the purpose in front of the City Hall for the benefit of the townspeople. True to the formal court pattern, at the end of the spectacle king and courtiers descended to the street and danced with the wives and daughters of the bourgeois. The king's company, of course, was all male, for by this time ladies did not appear with the gentlemen in the court ballets. They staged, from time to time, ballets of their own, but these were of comparatively minor importance.

It was Louis XIV, however, who was the greatest of all royal patrons of the dance, and during his reign the ballet reached new heights. The king was an excellent dancer and delighted in exhibiting his gifts. However outstanding they may have been, they led him to engage and to encourage the most brilliant of musicians, painters and poets to collaborate on his ballets. This was a fortunate thing for the future of the art, for it was Louis's sudden indifference in middle age (when his vanity would no longer allow him to exhibit his once shapely physique grown fat and puffy) that finally ended the long reign of the ballet as a court function. When he ceased to dance, the ballet lost its fashionable pre-eminence. But the very artists he had assembled about him to give it life were happily still at hand to see that it did not die.

THE BALLET BECOMES PROFESSIONAL

Chief among these able collaborators was Jean-Baptiste Lully, an Italian-born musician and dancer, who was not only a fine artist but an able and not too scrupulous politician. By the combination of his native gifts and guile he was able to use the ballet's crisis both to his personal advantage and to the enormous benefit of the art itself. By devious means he obtained the charter of the Royal Academy of Music, and with that organization he combined the Royal Academy of Dance which had been chartered some years earlier but had never functioned. His next stroke of policy was to persuade the king to turn over to him the magnificent theatre in the Palais Royal, built more than a generation before by Cardinal Richelieu, recently occupied by Molière and his company of actors and now made available by Molière's death. Here he started the ballet on its way as a professional art, alongside its musical twin from Italy, the opera, with a renewal of artistic principles such as it had not enjoyed since the days of the "Ballet Comique", and an ordering of technical method such as it had never had before.

Lully's major interest was musical, and his great contribution to the ballet at this period was his correlation of the two elements in a kind of theatrical unity. The specific dance department of the Academy was in the hands of his colleague, Pierre Beauchamps, likewise a musician and dancer of the court and also something of a genius. For many years the ideal of the classical culture of Greece and Rome had provided an example for the establishment of academies in the various arts and sciences, in which under royal decree could be set up rules and standards for practice. To Beauchamps now fell the opportunity to set up just such authoritative rules for the ballet. Here for the first time we find the five fundamental positions of the feet listed as such, as well as many other systematic developments, including a method of dance notation.

There could, indeed, have been no better time for such a first codification, for the ballet was undergoing changes which were destined to affect it in every conceivable way. The very theatre in which it was hereafter to be housed necessitated fundamental revisions in technical approach. Heretofore,

Late seventeenth century Italian stage with dancers. The scene is from Moniglia's "L'Ercole in Tebe."

in the court ballets, the dancers had entered at the end of the great hall and had had spectators on three sides of them; now that was no longer to be so. When Richelieu had built his theatre some thirty years before, he had followed the most modern pattern of the Italian theatre, which had long enjoyed leadership over the French in architectural innovations and machinery for the production of scenic spectacle. His theatre, accordingly, was built with an elevated stage on which all the action took place, framed by a proscenium arch, and the spectators sat directly in front of it, just as in our theatres of the present time. As a result, the dancer now would have nobody behind him or on either side of him, and had only to consider how he would look from one direction. It was incumbent upon him, then, to accept this established front as his focus. It was simple enough to keep his face toward his audience when he was moving forwards or backwards, but if he moved across the stage from side to side, it necessitated crossing one foot in front of the other, and with his feet in normal position this proved awkward. In order to do it expeditiously he found it advisable to rotate his hip joint so that the knee and toes pointed outwards instead of straight ahead. In this position the legs could be made to cross each other without interference. Similarly, if a dancer facing forward chose to raise his leg directly to the front, it would appear foreshortened to the spectator and the movement would have no design and only limited visibility. If, however, he rotated his hip outwards and raised his leg to the side, the movement could be seen in profile while he himself remained facing forward.

It would be erroneous to imply from all this that the turned-out hip was "invented" at this time, for it had certainly been in use to some extent, consciously or unconsciously, from time immemorial, both in and out of the dance. The very structure of the hip joint on the ball-and-socket pattern indicates the inherent serviceability of such a movement in everyday experience. Also, it must be remembered that the ballet itself had frequently played an incidental role on this very stage in the plays of Molière and the earlier productions of Cardinal Richelieu, not to speak of the theatres in Italy of similar type which had housed ballets to greater or less extent. The important aspect of the situation at this time is that now the ballet was on the road to being standardized on a professional basis, and that the practices dictated by the necessities of this particular theatre were shaping that official standardization. Thus it was that the principle of the turned-out hip now became for the first time a fundamental technical practice.

At this period, the rotation was not very extensive; the feet, when the heels were together, made scarcely more than a right angle. As the technical scope of the ballet increased over the years this angle was steadily widened until by the early nineteenth century it had become a full hundred and eighty degrees; that is, when the heels were together, the feet made a straight line with the toes pointing in opposite directions. This is one of the distinctive technical principles of the ballet, and a thoroughly logical one. It allows the legs to move freely in every direction and with a maximum of visibility from the spectator's angle of vision.

But if totally new forces had been brought to bear on the ballet, their influence was gradual. The tradition of courtliness on which it had been nurtured was not to be instantaneously overturned, and usages which had long since lost their original functions and whose meanings had been forgotten, were carried over unquestioningly into the new era by sheer inertia. Not until 1681, ten years after the establishment of Lully's academy, were women admitted to the company. As in the days of the court ballet, feminine roles had been danced by men. Masks, an ancient heritage from the ceremonial origins of dancing, continued to be worn by all dancers, both male and female. A kind of standard costume had also been adopted by the court, patterned after Renaissance ideas of the classic Greeks and Romans. The men were dressed according to what was believed to be the model of the Roman warrior, but what they actually wore consisted of high feathered headdress, ornate coat spreading at the waist into a "tonnelet" or stiff, hooped skirtlet virtually to the knees, knee breeches, gloves, stockings and heeled shoes. The women's dresses differed chiefly in the fact that their skirts were heavily panniered and reached the floor. The movement of the dance itself was fairly limited in scope and virtuosity, as was natural in an amateur art whose aims had been primarily toward elegance and display and whose costumes had accordingly hampered the body's activity considerably.

With the decline of these courtly aims and the growth of professionalism through the passing years, further changes were bound to occur, and a generation after the ballet had ceased to be an amateur art, we find an increased interest in virtuosity and the technical side of movement. This inevitably means that instead of concerning themselves with floor patterns, the dancers began to extend their movements upwards into the air, jumping, beating their feet together while off the ground, and generally giving the dance a concern with verticality where it had formerly been largely bound to horizontal design.

When there appears on the scene a feminine dancer who delights in these new technical matters, has a talent for elevation and can make a particularly effective use of crossing and recrossing her feet in the air (a figure which we have come to know as "entrechat"), it is clear that something will be done to alter the ladies' costume. Why waste all these skillful manoeuverings of the feet behind a long skirt which completely covers them? It is Marie-Anne de Cupis de Camargo, then, who takes the revolutionary step of shortening the dancer's skirt to the ankle. There is considerable scandal, to be sure, but the reform endures—a reform which is destined to be carried on in increasing measure over the centuries.

NOVERRE AND THE "BALLET OF ACTION"

Many reforms, indeed, of a more basic nature are due in the momentous eighteenth century, when the Renaissance had worn thin, when the culture of the ancients seemed far less important than the rational thinking of contemporary man, when theories of political democracy, freedom of conscience, and the general rights and potentialities of the individual, superseded the old reverence for self-constituted aristocracies and the authority of tradition. In every walk of life a new and revolutionary attitude toward human affairs was in the making, and as its natural accompaniment in the arts—those mediums through which are voiced the emotional experiences and aspirations of the times—there was a shift of emphasis away from formalism as an end in itself and toward the expression of human emotion and a reflection of life. The democratic revolution and the romantic revolution went hand in hand as manifestations of the same basic drive.

The Royal Academy of Music and Dance, supported by the crown and patronized by the nobility, was not likely by its background and character to be the most open field for such new and iconoclastic tendencies; but since, as we have already noted, movement is a medium highly sensitive to underlying and irrational emotional drives, the same issues that were growing in the life of the times at large found their expressions also in the dance, in spite of academic opposition.

A significant early figure in this new movement was Marie Sallé, a contemporary and arch-rival of Camargo. Her concern, unlike that of the brilliant virtuosa, was with dramatic realism and expressiveness. She, too, urged costume changes, but instead of being merely reforms as Carmago's changes were, hers were revolutionary. She wanted to abandon altogether the set uniform of the ballet and to dress each character in something that approached its own true style. Her ideas were vehemently opposed by the directors of the academy, and in order to give them expression she was forced to go to London. There she presented a ballet, "Pygmalion," in which as Galatea she put aside the conventional panniers and jeweled headdress and donned Greek draperies patterned after classic sculpture. To be sure, she wore them over her conventional corset and petticoats in a manner that to us is far from realistic, but for her own time it was a striking step forward toward representationalism. The experiment was a tremendous success and London flocked to see her, but her next venture (Handel's "Alcina," in which she attempted to dance the role of a boy) was unsuccessful, and she returned to Paris. Here her efforts were as unwelcome as before, and after a few unhappy seasons she retired from the ballet in disappointment.

But her ideas were not to die. A young man named Jean Georges Noverre was fired with the same enthusiasm, much of it no doubt lit directly by her, for though he was very young when she quit dancing, he often visited her in her retirement. His theory was much broader than hers and extended beyond costume to all aspects of the ballet, making it an independent theatre art instead of a mere decorative adjunct to opera. But though a generation had passed since Paris had rejected Sallé, the ballet was still completely hostile to Noverre. He perforce accepted positions as ballet master in other cities, and carried on, chiefly in Stuttgart, the evolution of what he called the "ballet d'action"; that is, the ballet in which the dance actually carries forward the dramatic action instead of simply interrupting it with pretty interludes as in the stereotyped practice then current.

He wanted dancing not only to arouse his admiration for its technical brilliance but to move him emotionally by its expressiveness just as drama and tragedy did. He demanded that the ballet become within its own medium an imitation of life. Like Sallé's notion of realism, Noverre's ideas seem to us far from realistic or expressive, but they constituted a revolutionary doctrine in their day. Though they were officially rejected at the Paris Opéra (now the home of the Royal Academy of Music and Dance), their influence crept into that sacrosanct institution anyhow, for many of its dancers were loyal admirers of Noverre. The use of the mask was abandoned, costuming was reformed to a certain extent, and the new concept of verisimilitude made itself felt. Eventually Noverre himself was actually accepted as ballet master at the Opéra, but by then his ideas were no longer novel. His tenure was brief and unhappily riddled by intrigues, of which he himself was by no means innocent, and he resigned.

The publication of his book, "Letters on the Dance and the Ballet," in 1761 was of paramount importance, for here he outlined his principles in a manner that made them available far beyond his sphere of personal influence and, indeed, beyond his own time. His ardent disciple, Dauberval, carried on his teachings with vigor in the south of France, (he was especially successful with the comic ballet, of which "La Fille Mal Gardée" is still occasionally performed in a late nineteenth century modernization), and Dauberval's pupil, Salvatore Viganó, developed them even further in Milan in the early nineteenth century. His critics, indeed, found that Viganó's "choreodrama" had taken dancing altogether out of the ballet and left it pure dramatic pantomime. With him the direct line from Noverre came to an end, but the principle of the "ballet d'action" had come to stay, and still prevails largely among us.

Meanwhile in Paris the French Revolution had wrought other changes in the ballet. Echoes of the contemporary world had found their way into the repertoire, and though the Greek gods and goddesses continued to dance in many ballets and still wore garb which was closer to the courtly uniform of Louis XIV's day than to the attire of the ancient Greeks, there were now ballets dealing with the sans-culottes of revolutionary Paris, others celebrating the American Revolution, and even such characters as priests and nuns were pictured in ballets protesting against religion and the church. The ancient tradition of dancing about lesser Greek classic personages such as nymphs and shepherds in poetic pastorals, now found itself reflecting the new democratic tone in works with contemporary peasants as their subjects.

As the nineteenth century dawned, there came still further reforms. The painter, David, deeply interested, as many of his colleagues had also recently become, in archeological accuracy, had persuaded his friend, Talma, the great tragic actor, to discard the old traditional style of reputedly Greek and Roman costuming which had persisted in the dramatic theatre as stubbornly as in the ballet. This astounding new "realism" was so successful that the ballet of necessity adopted it as well, and for a generation the ballet's still persistent Greeks disported themselves in tunics and chitons with some regard for authenticity.

Arthur Mahoney and Thalia Mara in reproductions of typical eighteenth century ballet costumes.

THE ROMANTIC REVOLUTION

But these were merely transitional steps leading to the truly revolutionary change which impended for the ballet. This was the birth of the romantic ballet. It was simply the culmination in the field of the dance of that total reorientation of thinking which is known as the Romantic Revolution. Like the parallel growth all through the eighteenth century of the social revolution which came to a head in the American war for independence and in the French Revolution, it was concerned with the inherent rights and potentialities of the "natural man" which the great thinkers of the Reformation had celebrated, and was opposed to social, political and religious hierarchies of all sorts.

So large was its scope and so radical its nature that it rivaled in importance even such a historical overturning as the Renaissance. The latter had touched chiefly the courtiers and the ruling classes, but the Romantic Revolution was a movement of the common people in both its political and its artistic manifestations. In effect it was a kind of counter-Renaissance. It repudiated the classical Graeco-Roman model which had been arbitrarily adopted by the Renaissance, and determined to pick up the direct road of progress from which it had deviated at the end of the Middle Ages. It renounced paganism for a return to Christian values; it demanded an end to the artist's slavery to the abstract and impersonal unities of classical culture and his freedom to treat instead of the moral conflicts of life. Victor Hugo became the spokesman for the entire movement when it had

Monsieur and Madame Achille, "from the Italian Opera House, Paris," as they appeared at the Bowery Theatre in New York in the early nineteenth century.

Marie Taglioni in "La Sylphide" from a highly fanci-
ful German print of the period.

reached its peak of artistic rebellion in the early nineteenth century, and his preface to his play,
"Cromwell," was a declaration of its principles. Here he demanded emancipation from the "despot-
ism of systems, codes and rule," and insisted that the true presentation of life consisted of both
beautiful and ugly, good and evil, elements in conflict.

The days of the classic Greeks were now over in the ballet; it was the picturesque Middle Ages
that intrigued its fancy as a model from the past. Indeed, a revival of that medieval mystic dualism
which pictured man as a creature always torn between the spirit and the flesh largely dominated the
scene. Supernatural creatures of the air fell in love with mortal men and came to tragic ends; dead
maidens rose from the grave to haunt unfaithful lovers; and in general there were moral victories
of the aerial and spiritual creatures over the earthly and sensual. If much of this seems mawkish
and sentimental to us (and, indeed, actually was so as the original impulse of the revolution
faded), it was nevertheless based on a vital emotional urge and had both inherent validity and
power.

In the interest of theatrical illusion in the ballet, it became customary to attach the dancers of
aerial roles to wires by which they could literally fly above the level of the stage. (This device was
already waiting to be used, for Didelot had created a sensation by introducing it purely as an in-
genious production novelty in his ballet, "Flore et Zéphire," in London in 1796.) But because
movement itself is automatically expressive of compelling emotional drives, this mechanical device
was not sufficient to satisfy it. The dancers, already able to leap into the air for brief moments of
suspension without artificial aids, now actually sought to sustain this quality of suspension in terms,
not of wires, but of their own movement. It is perhaps quite natural that in response to this desire
to inhabit the air they should have risen onto the points of their toes, even though at first they

A scene from "La Sylphide," the first "romantic" ballet.

were unable to remain there for any extended length of time. Thus out of a strong inner emotional compulsion this great technical innovation of dancing on the tips of the toes—the "pointes," as they are technically called—came about. Because it was so obviously right for its purpose, it was naturally developed, until with the aid of a reinforced shoe it could be transformed into a veritable new way of moving, suggestive of floating rather than walking, and to all intents ignoring the pull of gravity.

This new aerial style of moving came about so gradually that there is no record of who the first dancer was who danced on her "pointes," but it was probably introduced some time in the 1820's. Not until 1832 was the ballet presented that really crystalized the romantic style in general. This was "La Sylphide"—not to be confused with "Les Sylphides" created by Michel Fokine more than seventy years later. It was composed by Phillippe Taglioni for his daughter, Marie, and it told the story of a woodland creature of supernatural character who fell tragically in love with a Scotsman. For the costume of the nymph, the artist, Eugène Lamy, devised the full and filmy white skirt reaching halfway to the ankles which was destined to become almost as standard a costume for the ballerina as the old panniered dress of the court had been.

These ethereal ballets—sometimes referred to as "ballets blancs" or white ballets, because of the stageful of filmy-white-clad dancers they employed—were produced in profusion, and one of them actually survives in today's repertoire. This is "Giselle," created by Jean Coralli in 1841 for Carlotta Grisi. It has inevitably been altered with the passage of time; parts have been cut out because they seemed dull to later audiences, at least one important solo for the ballerina has been added in the first act, and the practice of suspending the dancers on wires in the supernatural scenes has been abandoned. But when it is danced by a great ballerina like Alicia Markova it still retains much of the flavor of the period.

44

Left: Fanny Elssler in "Sapateo de Cadiz," from an old music cover. Right: Carlotta Grisi in "Giselle."

Besides the mystic and supernatural qualities of ballets such as "Giselle" and "La Sylphide," the romantic ballet also contained elements of a very different sort. Since it was influenced by the ideology of democracy on the one hand and on the other hand was emotionally devoted to the Middle Ages, it could scarcely fail to find a new interest in both folk ways and the romantic problems of the lowly born. Peasant dances abounded in the supernatural ballets, and in addition, ballets of straight dramatic import about people of various exotic nationalities enjoyed a popularity of their own.

If Taglioni was the symbol of the mystical side of romanticism, the earthy side was equally symbolized by her rival and complete opposite, Fanny Elssler, who specialized in these more full-blooded romances. She was a Viennese woman of considerable beauty, as contrasted with Taglioni's marked lack of physical allure, and she danced with dramatic fire and personal charm altogether removed from her colleague's spiritual detachment. It was part of her practice to utilize in her ballets adaptations of folk dances such as the Italian tarantella, the Spanish cachuca, and dances from Russia and Poland. Elssler was the only one of the great galaxy of ballerinas of that day who ever came to America, and her two seasons in this country in the early '40's were phenomenally successful.

It is not surprising that a period which sentimentalized womanhood as the romantic period did should have raised the ballerina to an unprecedented height of esteem. This she was able to sustain in terms of technical accomplishment by her newly acquired ability to dance on her "pointes," which gave her a distinct advantage over her male colleague. Why he, too, was not expected to rise to the tips of his toes is explained only by the mental attitude of the time, which considered the woman as the spiritual type whose native element was the air and the man as her comparatively base and unaspiring consort. At any rate, the male dancer, poor soul, after having dominated the dance for centuries both by right of his superior social position in other days and by his greater athletic ability to leap and turn, found himself downright unpopular. He was apparently endured at all only because he was needed to support the ballerina in some of her more effective moments.

Quite naturally, with all these new artistic emphases and opportunities, the matter of technique became of increasing importance. But if Paris was still the artistic center of the ballet, it was indebted to Italy, as it had always been, for improvements of a technical sort. The summation of the new technical basis for this much broadened period of the ballet was to be found in the work of Carlo Blasis, Italian-born dancer who had danced in France and England and eventually returned to Milan as the greatest ballet master of the period. He re-codified the entire method and practice of the art, and established a system of training and education which to a large extent still prevails today.

This combination of artistic revitalization and technical organization made the 1830's and '40's a "golden age" of the ballet. So complete was its conquest over all traditions and accomplishments that had gone before it that it has come to be regarded by us as the virtual source and criterion of ballet practice. When we refer to the "classic ballet," it is this period and the styles and methods it established that we are thinking of, using the word "classic" not in its sense of referring to the ancient Greek culture but rather in the sense in which we apply it to the works of Shakespeare, Milton, Bach and Beethoven, as examples of an academically authoritative standard of excellence.

A scene from the Ballet Theatre revival of "Giselle" (1940) with Nana Gollner and Anton Dolin in central roles.

But as with every period of unusual inspiration, its finest impulses were eventually spent, and the innovations it had made were perpetuated only as empty surfaces with their original emotional motivations quite forgotten. The great inner urge of the time had been satisfied. The new technical range that was opened up was now increased and elaborated solely for its acrobatic potentialities. Dancing on the "pointes" lost all its spiritual significance and was treated simply as a means for providing an irreducibly small base for the ballerina to stand on while she performed miracles of balance and executed sequences of otherwise impossibly rapid turns.

The long, fluffy skirt which had been conceived as the poetic apparel of a creature of the air was now an unquestioned uniform. To be sure, it progressively shortened as time went on in order to facilitate the more and more involved technique, and ultimately it was reduced to little more than a puff of tulle around the hips. But certainly it did not indicate a supernatural creature any longer; it implied no characterization at all. If the ballerina was supposed to be a peasant maiden, she wore a little apron over it in front; if she was an ancient Greek, she had a key pattern on its edges; if she was a queen, she added jewels and a crown. Jewels she wore in any case, if she owned any, and her hair was dressed in the latest fashion of the day whether she was an Egyptian priestess or an American Indian. She also wore pink tights and slippers, irrespective of race or period, and danced on "pointes," employing the same basic vocabulary of steps and combinations for all roles.

Roland Guerard and Alicia Markova in the "Blue Bird" pas de deux from Petipa's "The Sleeping Beauty," danced as a separate divertissement with the Ballet Russe de Monte Carlo.

The general pattern of the late nineteenth century ballet became fairly set. The story was most likely a romance of the olden days. Frequently, as an inheritance from the mystical ways of the romantic ballet, it was a fairy tale. It was usually in three or four acts and lasted for a whole evening—including intermissions sometimes as long as forty-five minutes each in the Imperial Russian theatres, in order to allow the aristocrats in the audience to visit. Its plot was unfolded in terms of pantomime which consisted chiefly of a sign language of the hands, devoid of expressiveness and often unintelligible without the aid of program notes. The action was interrupted periodically by dance numbers, either by the soloists or by the corps de ballet in mass manoeuvres, without relation to the drama itself.

The climax of the evening was the "grand pas de deux" by the ballerina and her cavalier. It assumed a four-part form. The first part, called "adagio," consisted of slow and sustained movements in which the ballerina, supported by her partner throughout, was exhibited to her best advantage; the second was a solo or "variation" by the man; the third, a solo or "variation" by the ballerina; and the fourth, a "coda" in which the two danced together again, this time in rapid and brilliant movements.

The final act also usually contained a long succession of "divertissements," or specialty dances, by the various soloists of the cast in their roles as guests at a ball, villagers at a fête, entertainers before a king, or something of the sort.

Music was ordinarily turned out to order by staff musicians, who were merely instructed to

Right: Irina Baronova and Dimitri Romanoff in the Ballet Theatre revival of Dauberval's "La Fille Mal Gardée," staged by Bronislava Nijinska after the late nineteenth century revised version of the work long current in Russia. Opposite Page, Left: Alexandra Danilova and Frederic Franklin in the grand pas de deux from Ivanov's "The Nutcracker" with the Ballet Russe de Monte Carlo. Right: Igor Youskevitch and Tamara Toumanova in the grand pas de deux from "The Magic Swan," which is the third act of the Petipa-Ivanov "Swan Lake," presented by the Ballet Russe de Monte Carlo.

provide so many measures in 3/4 time, so many in 4/4, so many fast and so many slow passages. The scenery was similarly designed by staff artists along regulation lines. By and large, everything was subordinated to the technical virtuosity (and, of course, the feminine appeal) of the ballerinas.

For perhaps obvious reasons, not many of the ballets from this period survive in the popular repertoire today, except in the Russian theatres where many of them have been kept alive continuously as a traditional policy. The few exceptions are those which somehow escaped having scores by the usual hack musicians and have lived accordingly on the strength of their music. These include a much shortened version of "Coppelia," for which Delibes wrote one of the most charming of ballet scores; and the three Tchaikovsky ballets, "Swan Lake," "The Nutcracker" and "The Sleeping Beauty." None of these is given in its entirety as a rule; "Swan Lake" is reduced to its second act alone, "The Sleeping Beauty" has been made into several different arrangements of divertissements from its various acts under such titles as "Aurora's Wedding" and "Princess Aurora," and "The Nutcracker," greatly reduced, depends entirely upon its divertissements for its interest.

Of these four, only the earliest, "Coppelia," (1870), stems originally from Paris, though the form in which we know it is a made-over version from Russia in the '90's. The others were all direct products of Russia in the '90's, when the ballet in its time-honored homes in Italy and France was all but literally dead. It was sterile and vapid in Russia, as well, but it was from Russia that the next great impulse to life sprang. Though it was rejected and suppressed in its own land, it served once again to revivify the art in the western world.

FOKINE REAWAKENS THE BALLET

The ballet came to Russia first as part of that mass importation of western culture begun by Peter the Great. In 1735 the Empress Anna established an academy and it has existed ever since under all the Czars and on into the Soviet regime under the patronage and administration of the state. Though this was fairly late in the history of the art, the finest of masters were imported from France and Italy and enormous sums of money were lavished upon it by one of the world's wealthiest courts. There were years of particular growth under Catherine the Great; then Catherine's son, Paul I, summoned Charles Louis Didelot to take charge in 1801, and it was well on the way to being the best ballet anywhere in the world and probably the most splendid.

But it remained an importation. All through the nineteenth century, though it produced ever finer dancers out of its own ranks, it continued to be directed by French and Italian masters and to bestow most of the stellar roles upon celebrated foreign artists—until, indeed, the decline of the art in western Europe left no celebrated artists to bestow them upon. Possibly because of the continued subsidy and direction of the imperial house during these lean artistic years, the ballet in Russia maintained a far higher standard than existed in other countries where royal patronage had long since ceased. But from the standpoint of vitality and that inward urgency that produces artistic progress, it was as lean in Russia as elsewhere.

Actually there were important stirrings under the surface among the artists, but in so strictly regulated an organization, murmurings of discontent from below had a hard time reaching the surface, and even when they succeeded in doing so, they received short shrift. It was in 1904 that there came the first artistic expression of rebellion. This was in the form of a letter to the directors by a gifted young Russian of 24, who had been graduated from the academy with distinction six years previously, had stepped immediately into the dancing of important roles in the company, was a teacher of some of the junior classes now, himself, and

Michel Fokine in his own ballet, "Cléopâtre" (1908).

50

Right: Thamar Karsavina in her original role in "Pé-trouchka" and Adolph Bolm as the Blackamoor. The work was first produced in 1911. Below: Tatiana Riabouchinska and corps de ballet in the Ballet Russe de Monte Carlo revival of Fokine's "Les Sylphides." The work was first produced at the Imperial Ballet School in St. Petersburg in 1908.

Left: Lucia Chase and Leon Danielian in Fokine's own revival of his "Carnaval" for Ballet Theatre in 1940. The original production was at a charity performance in St. Petersburg in 1910. Below: Scene from the Ballet Russe de Monte Carlo revival of "Pétrouchka."

Adolph Bolm in his own revival of "Pétrouchka" at the Metropolitan Opera House, New York.

had a desire to become a composer of ballets. His name was Michel Fokine, and the letter, which was in the main a request to be allowed to create a specific ballet, denounced the sterility of contemporary practices and outlined a specific program for reforming them. It is one of the most important documents in the history of the art, but its receipt by the directors was never even acknowledged. The only result it produced was a bulletin instructing singers in the opera no longer to interrupt the action by taking bows after their arias.

Fokine's ideas, of course, went much deeper than the business of operatic bowing. They were essentially a restatement of the same principles which Noverre had preached nearly a hundred and fifty years earlier, now enriched by the knowledge and cultural evolution of the intervening generations, and the personal urgency of an artist of genius. Like Noverre, Fokine wanted to make the ballet an expressive art, a mirror of life comparable to the drama. The five major planks of his platform for reforming the current stereotyped methods were: first, that the use of ready-made movements, right out of the academic classroom, should be abandoned on the stage, and every ballet should have a style of movement suitable to the country and period in which its action was laid; second, that the entire dramatic action should unfold continuously in terms of movement instead of consisting of scenes in pantomime to relate the plot, interrupted by meaningless dance numbers of entirely unrelated character; third, that the conventional sign-language, which was known as pantomime and was totally unintelligible even to dancers playing a scene together,

53

Above, left: Maria Tallchief and Yurek Lazowski in the Ballet Russe de Monte Carlo revival of Fokine's "Schéhérazade." The original production was in 1911. Right: Thamar Karsavina and Adolph Bolm in Fokine's "Thamar" (1912). Below: Irina Baronova and Paul Petroff in the DeBasil Ballet Russe revival of Fokine's "Le Spectre de la Rose," first produced in 1911.

should be discarded, and that the entire body of the dancer should be expressive at all times; fourth, that not just the soloist but the whole company should be used to forward the dramatic theme and to be expressive, instead of keeping the corps de ballet for purely decorative interludes which served only to allow the principals to get their breath or to change their costumes; fifth, that the music should be no longer a mere succession of little dance numbers, but should be a unity carrying forward the dramatic action just as the dancing did, that the scenery should similarly be creative in style just as the movement style should be creative, and that the costumes should no longer be held to the tradition of ballet skirt, pink tights and toe slippers, but should accurately reflect the style of the country and period in which the action was set. The whole work should involve the active collaboration of choreographer, musician and designer.

He considered the academic technique indispensable for teaching but not an adequate

Michel Fokine and Vera Fokina in "Daphnis and Chloe" (1912).

vocabulary for artistic expression; he found it foolish for the ancient Greeks to be pictured dancing on "pointes" instead of in their historically accurate bare feet; "pointes" he returned to the supernatural or purely imaginary characters for whom they were originally designed.

It has frequently been said that Fokine's reforms were inspired by Isadora Duncan, who at that period had begun to startle the artistic world with her radical approach to the dance, but this theory is untenable. Fokine's ideas had begun to take shape before he had ever seen Isadora dance (she did not appear in Russia until 1905), and were fundamentally quite different. They are far closer to Noverre's, of which, indeed, they are a virtual fulfillment. He unquestionably admired Isadora, was influenced by her in a measure and encouraged by her insurgency, but the goals at which the two of them were driving had little in common. To the end of his life, Fokine, with his deeply rooted ethnological conviction of style, persisted in considering Isadora to be a mistress of the classic Greek style and nothing more, completely overlooking the quite opposite emphasis of her art on purely subjective expression. Whatever similarity existed between the two artists was due to the fact that they were both sensitive creators animated by the same emotional drive that was at work in the world at large. These years marked the beginnings of what has come to be known as the modern movement, and Fokine and Isadora felt its urgency in their own terms, just as the musician Debussy, the painter Cézanne, the architect Frank Lloyd Wright, felt it in theirs.

THE BALLET RUSSE IN THE WESTERN WORLD

That modern impulses should find their way into so traditional an institution as the imperial theatres of Russia was unthinkable. Many of Fokine's colleagues, especially the younger ones, were enthusiastic about his ideas, but the only opportunities he had to put them into operation were on private and semi-private occasions such as benefits and students' performances. Even here, when he attempted to put his Greeks in bare feet, he was forced to accept the ridiculous compromise of dressing them in pink tights with toes painted on them.

But the force of the revolt continued to grow within the company, and the directors of the institution no doubt greeted with relief an opportunity that now presented itself to allow the excited rebels to work off their enthusiasm at a safe distance from the home organization. Serge Diaghileff, formerly attached to the direction in an administrative capacity, asked leave to borrow the insurgents during their long summer vacation for a season in Paris. It was a fine solution all the way round, and in 1909 Paris saw "Russian Ballet" for the first time. Probably no other artistic event of modern times has ever made so deep and so instantaneous an impression. The news was published around the world and a new era began for the art of the ballet.

Because of the outbreak of World War I in 1914, these annual Paris seasons during the summer vacations of the dancers from St. Petersburg and Moscow were few in number, but they served to revivify a moribund art. Fokine's ideas had free rein at last; he had the full collaboration of such painters as Benois and Bakst, and such a musician as Stravinsky, plus the use of music by Chopin, Rimsky-Korsakoff, Schumann, and other composers whose work had never been turned to dance purposes before Isadora's time; his company of dancers included Karsavina, Bolm, Nijinsky, and for one season, Pavlova. (Fokine, himself, though his fame as a choreographer has overshadowed his career as a performer, was also a dancer of exceptional ability.)

Half a dozen of the standard masterpieces of today's repertory were introduced to Paris during these years—"Les Sylphides," "Carnaval," "Pétrouchka," "Schéhérazade," "Prince Igor" and "Le

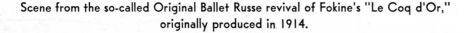

Scene from the so-called Original Ballet Russe revival of Fokine's "Le Coq d'Or,"
originally produced in 1914.

Above: Irina Baronova as the Queen of Shemakhan in "Le Coq d'Or." Above right: Tatiana Riabouchinska in the title role of "Le Coq d'Or." Right: Igor Youskevitch and Mia Slavenska in the Ballet Russe de Monte Carlo revival of Fokine's "Les Elfes," originally produced in 1924.

Spectre de la Rose;" not to mention "The Fire-bird," "Thamar," "Daphnis and Chloe," "Le Coq d'Or" "Cléopâtre," "Le Pavillon d'Armide," and others whose success was shorter lived for one reason or another.

It is practically impossible for us today to judge of the true importance of these works, for as they exist in the repertoires of the various companies, they are mere shadows of their original incarnations. Not only are the companies, especially as regards the ensembles, inferior to the magnificent group from the Imperial Ballet which first performed them, but the ballets themselves have been largely forgotten and handed around by memory from one ballet master to another.

This is perhaps more unfortunately true of "Pétrouchka" than any of the others; once an epoch-making work which introduced a stylization of psychologically expressive movement into the ballet for the first time, it is now generally an ill-acted, shabbily rehearsed piece, in which supernumeraries, hired for the performance, walk on in the many vital crowd scenes without form or direction. "Schéhérazade" though not so significant a work to begin with, has deteriorated to the same extent and in many of the same particulars. The ballet which fares best is "Les Sylphides," mainly because it utilizes the standard academic vocabulary of movement which all ballet companies know (it was created as a sentimental memory of the period of Tag-

Top: Scene from Fokine's "Don Juan" as presented by René Blum's Ballets de Monte Carlo in 1936. Middle: Scene from Fokine's "Cinderella" as presented by the Original Ballet Russe in 1940. Bottom: Anton Dolin and Irina Baronova in Fokine's "Bluebeard" as presented by the Ballet Theatre in 1941.

lioni), but also partly because Fokine himself restaged it superbly as late as 1940 for the Ballet Theatre in New York, giving it more rehearsals than even the original production had had.

The mere passing of time has dimmed their revolutionary aspects; the breathtaking fire and native color of the warriors' dances in "Prince Igor" have become commonplace; the subject matter and the costuming of "Schéhérazade" are no longer daring; what was once a completely new approach has long since been accepted as the basis of general practice. A new generation of reformers has arisen, indeed, to rebel against it as already old-fashioned, and to lead the art ahead in further advances. We cannot, therefore, expect to share the emotional impact that was produced by Fokine's early ballets upon their time; we must inevitably look upon them as masterpieces of another era, milestones of progress which only yesterday were passed on the road of the ballet to ever-increasing achievement.

After the great days of Diaghileff's company, Fokine continued to create for other companies in other parts of the world with the same skill and the same basic artistic convictions until the time of his death in 1942. Among the works of these later years which are still active in the repertoires of various organizations are "Les Elfes," "Don Juan," "L'Epreuve d'Amour," "Cinderella," "Paganini," and "Bluebeard."

Scene from Fokine's "Paganini" as presented by the Original Ballet Russe in 1940.

PAVLOVA AND NIJINSKY

The two outstanding personalities among the dancers who emerged from the period when the Russian ballet made itself known outside its own country for the first time were, of course, Anna Pavlova and Vaslav Nijinsky. Pavlova was one of the earliest supporters of Fokine in his agitations for reform. For her he composed "The Swan" to be danced at a benefit way back in 1905, and she appeared in "Les Sylphides," "Le Pavillon d'Armide" and "Cléopâtre" in the first Paris season. But she was not sympathetic to Diaghileff's ideas in general, and early disassociated herself from his group to tour with a company of her own, as she had done, indeed, under Adolph Bolm's direction in Scandinavia before the Diaghileff project had been launched. Her art was unsympathetic to the modern experimentations which animated the Diaghileff group; its kinship was rather with the spirit of Taglioni, broadened and enriched, but unaltered in substance. A dramatic actress of wonderful eloquence in movement, and an exquisite stylist, she carried forward the essential tradition of the romantic ballet.

She was not a choreographer herself, having composed only one ballet, "Autumn Leaves"; the company with which she frequently surrounded herself and many of the works she appeared in were scarcely worthy of her genius, and she contributed nothing to the advancement of the ballet in new directions, but the perfection of her personal art was such that in her touring of the world over many years she made undoubtedly more converts to the art of the ballet than any other artist has ever done.

Nijinsky, except for his status as an artist, belongs at the opposite end of the scale. A protégé, both personal and professional, of Diaghileff from almost the beginning of his career, he was deeply concerned with the modern directions of his art and created some highly revolutionary chore-

Right: Anna Pavlova in "Snowflakes."

Opposite page: Anna Pavlova in a Greek dance. Alexandre Volinine, Laurent Novikoff and Anna Pavlova in "Les Coquetteries de Columbine."

ography. His "Sacre du Printemps," for example, found not even his patron, the radical Diaghileff, in sympathy. He was perhaps the finest male dancer the ballet has ever known (if such things can be measured over the passing centuries), not only for his technical accomplishments, which included especially spectacular elevation, but also for his powers as an actor. In this latter capacity, he was declared by Sarah Bernhardt, after she had seen his performance of "Pétrouchka," to be the greatest actor in the world. This aspect of his art is frequently overshadowed by his more startling ability to leap, which has become legendary, but it is ultimately of greater substance.

In spite of his worldwide fame, Nijinsky's career lasted slightly less than ten years from the time of his debut with the Imperial Ballet in St. Petersburg in the spring of 1908. Even a very considerable part of this brief period found him inactive, for his relations with Diaghileff were broken off summarily upon his marriage in the fall of 1913, he danced hardly at all between that time and the outbreak of the war, and he was then interned as an enemy alien in Austria. He was not released from this detention until 1916, when he joined the Diaghileff company (or what was left of it) in its first North American tour, and after one more season in the Americas, he returned to Europe where he was committed to an insane asylum shortly afterwards.

His dancing must obviously remain in the field of legend. Of the four ballets he created as choreographer, only "L'Après-midi d'un Faune" survives, and that in a form that bears the faintest possible relationship to the original. "Le Sacre du Printemps," the cause of a riot in the theatre at its première, received only six performances; "Jeux" fared scarcely better; and "Tyl Eulenspiegel," produced in New York, was abandoned almost at once.

On the face of the evidence, therefore, his lasting contribution to the ballet would seem to consist of nothing more tangible than the inspiration of a vivid creative personality as it flashed across the scene. It is possible, however, to believe that in his choreography for "Le Sacre du Printemps"

he opened the way for a radical use of creative movement which the ballet had never seen before and which was nearer to the attitude of the modern dance than the ballet. Fokine had turned against the established vocabulary of the classic ballet and had insisted that certain specific styles—Spanish, Greek, Russian and the like—should be substituted for it according to the subject of the particular work. In "Pétrouchka" he had gone further and made the movements of his three chief characters, who were all puppets, an exaggerated and puppetlike expression of their human psychological types. But in "Le Sacre" Nijinsky went still further; disregarding Fokine's advocacy of ethnological styles and his one step toward psychological style, Nijinsky used purely invented movement which grew out of his personal reaction to the savage music of Stravinsky and the prehistoric subject of the ballet. He actually denied the teachings of the academic ballet, used the toes violently turned in, heavy movements, short phrases, angular and broken lines. Certainly the ballet world was not ready for any such modernism in 1913; but if Nijinsky's career had continued, it is likely that he would have persisted in his demand for unlimited freedom in the use of movement, irrespective of whether it conformed to any existing style or system, and the subsequent history of the ballet might have been altogther different.

Vaslav Nijinsky (left) as Pétrouchka; (center) in his own ballet, "L'Après-midi d'un Faune (1912); and (right) as the favorite slave in "Schéhérazade."

The first world war brought to a definite end the purely Russian period of the Ballet Russe in Western Europe. Not only were many of the leading artists cut off from each other in various countries but Diaghileff's access to the great state schools and companies was forever ended by the Russian Revolution. It was up to him to proceed henceforth on an entirely different basis. The company was now not even informally an offshoot of the Imperial Ballet, but his own enterprise to do with as he pleased.

Little by little its character was transformed into something that reflected his own tastes ever more clearly. Its dancing personnel remained predominantly Russian but no longer exclusively so. The list of composers and painters now included, besides Larionov and Stravinsky, who were as international in taste as Diaghileff himself, such names as Poulenc, Auric, Milhaud, Satie, de Falla, Laurencin, Picasso, Dérain, Pruna, Rouault. The general flavor, no longer Russian, became that of the international art movement which centered in Paris. Experimentation, in which Diaghileff delighted for its own sake, flourished, particularly in the fields of music and décor. Since money was always scarce in spite of Diaghileff's skill at raising it, great ingenuity had to be practiced to reconcile artistic necessity with limited means, and this only added to the experimentation. The company's home was no longer St. Petersburg but Monte Carlo, where it played an annual season, gave many of its premières, and spent much of its rehearsal time and its leisure. The male dancer

Left: Alexandra Danilova and Leonide Massine in his "Boutique Fantasque" (1919). **Right:** Leonide Massine, with Sophie Pflanz and L. Klementowitch, in his first ballet, "Soleil de Nuit" (1915).

assumed pre-eminence, usurping the place that had been held so long by the ballerina, since Diaghileff was innately indifferent to feminine charms.

For the first time in its long history, the ballet, heretofore always stultified by the stuffiness of royal patronage, was officially encouraged to be daring, unconventional and novel. As long as Diaghileff lived, his company, for better or worse, was in the very forefront of the "avant garde."

LEONIDE MASSINE

During the years between the war and Diaghileff's death in 1929, three choreographers shared the responsibility of creating the repertory, namely, Leonide Massine, Bronislava Nijinska and George Balanchine.

Much the greater part of it fell to Massine, whose expert craftsmanship was largely responsible for carrying the company forward during the first years after the war. He had been discovered by Diaghileff as a young student at the drama school in Moscow, and had been brought into the company at the age of seventeen to be developed into a successor to Nijinsky when the latter was dismissed by Diaghileff for having married. He danced his first leading role in 1914 in "La Légende de Joseph," created for him by Fokine, and he choreographed his own first ballet, "Soleil de Nuit," in 1915.

Leonide Massine, Leon Woizikowski and David Lichine in the Ballet Russe de Monte Carlo revival of Massine's "Les Matelots," first produced in 1925.

Below: Scene from Massine's "Jeux d'Enfants" (1933). Scene from Massine's "Scuola di Ballo" (1933). Right: Serge Lifar in Massine's "Ode" (1928), his last ballet for Diaghileff. Below right: Tamara Toumanova and Leonide Massine in the Ballet Russe de Monte Carlo revival of his "Tricorne," first produced in 1919.

Above: Scene from "Le Beau Danube," revised by Massine in 1933 for the Ballet Russe de Monte Carlo from his earlier version for Count Etienne de Beaumont in 1924. Below: Alexandra Danilova and Leonide Massine in "Le Beau Danube."

Both his style as a dancer and his approach to choreography show his early leaning toward the dramatic stage. He has always exhibited, for example, one of the rarest gifts of a dancer, which is, paradoxically enough, the ability to stand still effectively on the stage, and he has a genuine flair for characterization, particularly in comedy roles. Most of his ballets, especially those created during the years with Diaghileff, are devoted to storytelling, usually on comedy themes and dealing with farcical characters. "Boutique Fantasque," "The Three-Cornered Hat" ("Tricorne"), and, less frequently, "The Good-Humored Ladies," are still to be seen in the repertoire of contemporary companies, and works of the same general type which date from after Diaghileff's death include "Le Beau Danube," "Gaîté Parisienne" and the occasionally presented "Scuola di Ballo."

A more serious and a more abstract trend was early indicated in his restaging, along totally different lines from Nijinsky's, of "Le

Nina Verchinina and corps de ballet in the first of Massine's symphonic ballets, "Les Présages" (1933).

David Lichine and Irina Baronova in Massine's "Beach" (1933).

Sacre du Printemps." This trend really began to become important to him toward the end of Diaghileff's regime in such works as "Le Pas d'Acier" and "Ode," in both of which, however, he was also concerned to a considerable extent with the use of stage mechanics along with movement for the creation of his effects. His full tendency toward the abstract ballet came about after Diaghileff's time in his turning to visualizations of symphonic music, generally with symbolic dramatic programs for the action—"Les Présages," set to the Fifth Symphony of Tchaikovsky; "Choreartium," set to the Fourth Symphony of Brahms; "Seventh Symphony" to Beethoven's music; "Symphonie Fantastique" to Berlioz's; "Rouge et Noir" to the First Symphony of Shostakovich.

Perhaps his most distinguished work, though one that has not proven to be a box-office favorite, falls into none of these categories; it is "Nobilissima Visione" (renamed in this country "St. Francis"), a kind of biography in medieval terms, with music by Paul Hindemith and décor by Pavel Tchelitchev. Here again Massine's feeling for the dramatic theatre stands him in good stead as both choreographer and dancer.

Above: Irina Baronova in "Les Présages." Below: Tatiana Riabouchinska in "Choreartium."

Above left: Irina Baronova, Tamara Toumanova, Leonide Massine and others in Massine's "Union Pacific" (1934). Above right: Scene from Massine's "Choreartium" (1933). Lower right: Nini Theilade in Massine's "Saint Francis" (1938)

BRONISLAVA NIJINSKA

Bronislava Nijinska, separated from the Diaghileff company by the war in 1914, returned seven years later to prove herself not only the excellent dancer she had formerly been but also for the first time an equally distinguished choreographer. During her three or four years as chief creator of ballets for the company she produced, among other things, two works of major importance.

The first was "Les Noces," which she treated in a manner that neither Diaghileff nor Stravinsky approved of in advance, and which caused almost as much public antagonism as her brother's "Sacre" had done. Set to Stravinsky's revolutionary music scored for pianos, percussion and voices, it was a primitive Russian wedding ceremonial, with starkly simple scenery and an unornamented, architectural use of movement, largely by solid groups of dancers. There was a marked kinship here to her brother's use of purely invented movement for expressive purposes, though in a more ordered and less violent form. Of particular interest was her employment of "pointes," not for aerial illusion or for conventional acrobatic effect, but as an instrumentality for expression in a highly stylized idiom. Her peasant maidens did not so much rise onto the tips of their toes as dig them into the earth with a kind of inarticulate, archaic passion. The work was seen in the United States in 1936 in a revival by the De Basil Ballet Russe, and proved to be still unpopular with the general public for all its actual distinction. Its performance was inadequate, however, for the dancers had no fundamental grasp of the work and were unused to such an original approach to movement, which was nearer to the modern dance than to the ballet. It remains, nevertheless, one of the great works of the modern repertoire.

The second ballet of outstanding importance which she contributed to the Diaghileff repertoire was "Les Biches," a highly sophisticated and satirical picture of the decadent social life of its time (1924), without any specific plot. Its value lay once again in its original comment. As in her use of "pointes" in "Les Noces," Nijinska here employed the elements of the academic ballet to deny its own traditional style and to achieve a piquant contemporary expressiveness. She herself considered this ballet as establishing a new essential approach to a vocabulary of movement for the modern ballet just as "La Sylphide" had established an essential approach for the lush romantic period.

Neither this nor any of the other works she created for Diaghileff, except "Les Noces," has been performed in this country. New York has seen briefly a reproduction of the Ravel "Bolero" which was done first for Ida Rubinstein in Paris, the Bach "Etude" as she finally revised it for her own Théâtre de Danse in Paris in 1932, the "Chopin Concerto" which she made for the Polish Ballet, and the light and brilliant "Cent Baisers" done for the De Basil Ballet Russe. In all these compositions are evident her grasp of form, her distinctive style in movement and her rich inventiveness. But these constitute only a small cross section of her major work. For the most part, what she has done in this country has been in the minor category.

Left: Alicia Markova and George Skibine in Massine's "Aleko" (1942). Center: Alicia Markova in Massine's "Rouge et Noir" (1939). Right: Tamara Toumanova, André Eglevsky and others in a scene from the surrealist "Labyrinth" (1941).

BALANCHINE AND AMERICAN BALLET

The third member of Diaghileff's choreographic triumvirate was George Balanchine, who did not join the company until late in its life. His education had been begun in the old Imperial Russian academy in St. Petersburg and had continued there after the Revolution. But his new and radical ideas about choreography found no encouragement whatever in official circles, for the State Ballet remained as bound by traditionalism under the soviets as under the czars. As a result, Balanchine, after some effort, got permission to go to western Europe, taking with him several of his colleagues (among them Alexandra Danilova) who agreed with his artistic ideas. Diaghileff apparently found his approach congenial at once, took him and his companions into the company, and when Nijinska vacated the post of choreographer in 1925, put him into it.

Of the ten ballets he created for the company before its dissolution at Diaghileff's death, only one has been seen in this country, "Apollon Musagète," retitled "Apollo" in the repertory of the Ballet Theatre. It is true that a version of "La Chatte" was presented here by Serge Lifar, but Balanchine completely disowned it as being false to his original creation. Works composed for other European companies, however, which have been performed here include "La Concurrence," "Cotillon," "Errante," "Songes," and "Mozartiana."

In 1933 he was brought to New York by Lincoln Kirstein to organize and head the American Ballet, and his work has become widely known in this country by his productions for that company, the Ballet Theatre and especially the Ballet Russe de Monte Carlo, not to mention his numerous contributions to theatrical productions and motion pictures. "Serenade," "Ballet Imperial," "Baiser de la Fée," "Danses Concertantes," "Concerto Barocco," and "Waltz Academy" are among his more popular creations during this period; and "Balustrade," set to the Stravinsky violin concerto, and "Orpheus," a production of Gluck's opera with the singers seated in the orchestra pit, are perhaps the most experimental and controversial

Left: Scene from Balanchine's "Apollon" as revived by the American Ballet in 1937. His first production, under the title of "Apollon Musagète," was for Diaghileff in 1928. Right: Serge Lifar in Balanchine's "Le Fils Prodigue" (1929)

Top left: Tamara Touma-
nova in "La Concur-
rence." Top center:
Frederic Franklin and
Alexandra Danilova in Ba-
lanchine's "Mozartiana"
in a revival by the Ballet
Russe de Monte Carlo of
the work originally pro-
duced in 1933. Top right:
Irina Baronova in "La
Concurrence." Center
right: Scene from Balan-
chine's "Cotillon" (1932).
Lower right: Scene from
Balanchine's "La Concur-
rence" (1932).

Above left: Scene from Balanchine's "The Card Party,"
as produced by the Ameri-
can Ballet in 1937. Above
right: Scene from the Ballet
Russe de Monte Carlo re-
vival of Balanchine's "Ballet
Imperial," first produced by
the American Ballet in 1942.
Right: Lew Christensen in
Balanchine's "Orpheus"
(1936).

Above left: Lubov Roudenko and Igor Youskevitch in the Ballet Russe de Monte Carlo revival of "The Card Party." Above center: Ruthanna Boris and Nicolas Magallanes in Balanchine's "Serenade," first produced in 1934. Above right: Mia Slavenska and André Eglevsky in the Ballet Russe de Monte Carlo revival of Balanchine's "Baiser de la Fée," first presented by the American Ballet in 1937. Left: Lew Christensen and Annabelle Lyon in "Orpheus."

Balanchine's ballets concern themselves very rarely with story, and are nearer in substance to musical compositions than dramatic. Frequently, indeed, they are inspired by and actually built on the form of specific musical compositions. He is himself a trained musician and pianist, so that this attitude toward music is easy to understand. His workmanship as a composer is deft and formally skillful, and his love of novelty has led him into wide inventiveness in movements, group arrangement and acrobatic lifts, though his basic idiom is strictly that of the classic school. He is concerned with the ballet not as an expressive medium but rather as an absolute aesthetic one, and in this neo-classic field he is the undisputed leader. The style he has evolved—not at all didactically or self-consciously—is a highly individual one, characterized by clean line, simplicity of bearing, and a strongly piquant, if predominantly lyric, flavor. By many ballet enthusiasts he is regarded as the outstanding contemporary master of his art.

Balanchine occupies an especially strategic position in this country. Because of both the soundness of his background and the particular character of his creative approach, he was chosen by Kir-

Right: Scene from Balanchine's "Danses Concertantes" (1944). Lower left: Maria Tallchief, Nicolas Magallanes and Mary Ellen Moylan in "Danses Concertantes." Lower center: Nathalie Krassovska in "Le Bourgeois Gentilhomme." Lower right: Fernando Alonso, Albia Kavan and Harold Lang in Balanchine's "Waltz Academy" (1944).

stein as the key figure in a long-term plan to establish the ballet as part of the artistic life of America. Looking at history, Kirstein saw that the Italian roots of the art had been transplanted to France and supported there in such a manner that they eventually blossomed into a specifically French art; that these Italian-French roots in turn, transplanted to Russia and nurtured there, had flowered into still another and more brilliant manifestation, colored by the Russians' particular gifts as a people. If these Italo-Franco-Russian roots could be transplanted to America and once more encouraged to acclimate themselves to a new environment, there seemed no reason to believe that a specifically American form of ballet should not emerge in due time. To that end he set up not only a producing company, but what was more basic, a school, properly financed and organized as a non-profit educational institution, to serve as the nearest practicable equivalent, in a strongly competitive field, of an official academy. Thus, when and if this well-conceived dream evolves into its ultimate reality, Balanchine will occupy a position similar to that of the Italian Lully in the foundation of the French ballet, and of the French Didelot in the foundation of the Russian.

Group from Balanchine's "Le Bourgeois Gentilhomme" (1944).

A NON-RUSSIAN ERA DAWNS

Since the death of Diaghileff, no figure has risen to dominate the field as he did. The personnel and the ideas that survived him have been dispersed among several rapidly shifting organizations, differing chiefly in business and financial arrangements, and not at all in artistic principles. They have employed largely the same dancers and choreographers, have claimed Monte Carlo as their headquarters at one time or another, have sued each other in the courts over rights to works which belong equally well in any of their repertoires, and in general are undistinguishable from each other in creative aims. There is no point, then, in considering the organizational differences which have divided the post-Diaghileff Ballet Russe into such separate bodies as the Ballets de Monte Carlo, Ballet Russe de Monte Carlo, Col. W. de Basil's Ballets Russes de Monte Carlo, Original Ballet Russe, and so forth.

It is evident, indeed, that the Russian Ballet as such is a declining influence. The Soviet schools and theatres have clung to the old practices against which Fokine long ago rebelled; the important figures who belong to that memorable advance on the western world in 1909 or were later developed in the line of that bright tradition under Diaghileff, are few and scattered, and there is no longer any parent wing to shelter young potential bearers of the heritage. The future of the art must look to other sources, all of them fundamentally influenced by the forces unleashed by Fokine,

Left: David Lichine and Tatiana Riabouchinska in Lichine's "Graduation Ball" (1940). Below: Alexandra Danilova in Frederick Ashton's ballet, "The Devil's Holiday" (1939).

Above left: Vera Zorina in David Lichine's "Helen of Troy" (1943). Above right: Mia Slavenska in "The Magic Swan." Lower left: Tamara Toumanova. Lower right: Irina Baronova.

Alicia Markova in (left) "The Nutcracker" (below left) "Giselle" (below right) Leonide Massine's "Don Domingo" (1942)

but none of them in the direct line of descent.

In England, long an enthusiastic center for the importation of Russian ballet, important steps have been taken toward the establishment of the art on a native basis. The leader of the movement is Ninette de Valois, Irish born in spite of her nom de théâtre, who has long been an independent thinker and indefatigable worker. Though in 1923 she won the then high honor of a place in the Diaghileff company, she remained only for two seasons, preferring to carry forward her own ideas. To this end she established a school and produced her ballets where and as she could.

As a result of these experiments, she was invited in 1935 by Lilian Baylis, director of the Old Vic and Sadler's Wells Theatres, to install ballet in these virtually national theatres, and from small beginnings the project grew to its present impressive dimensions. The Sadler's Wells Ballet has been for some time a permanent institution giving regular performances and increasing steadily in prestige and accomplishment. Now at the close of the war, it has moved from its former comparatively small quarters into the capacious ones of Covent Garden, where it can meet comparison with the best ballets of the day in the matter of production facilities, orchestra, personnel and repertory.

Associated with Miss de Valois as choreographer is Frederick Ashton, and during the war years Robert Helpmann has risen from the ranks to take his place also in this department. Most of the important British dancers, including

Top: Scene from Kurt Jooss's "Impressions of a Big City" (1932). Center: Scene from Kurt Jooss's "The Green Table" (1932). Below: Scene from Kurt Jooss's "A Ball in Old Vienna" (1932).

Alicia Markova and Anton Dolin, have appeared at one time or another in its productions. In order to devote herself entirely to the direction of the now truly enormous enterprise, Miss de Valois has announced her intention of retiring from the field of choreography after the production of her new "Joan of Arc." It is an open secret that as soon as she has rehabilitated her company after its wartime hardships, she will make an American tour with it.

Above: Scene from Frederick Ashton's "Horoscope" (1938). Below: Scene from Frederick Ashton's "Les Patineurs," for the Sadler's Wells company (1937). Opposite page: Michael Somes, June Brae and Richard Ellis in Ninette de Valois's "Checkmate" (1937).

ANTONY TUDOR AND NEO-ROMANTICISM

Also out of England has come one of the most imposing figures in the contemporary ballet, Antony Tudor, who has made perhaps a deeper impression outside his native country than in it. More than any other choreographer, he has taken up the tradition of expressiveness in the ballet where Fokine left it and has carried it forward into new dimensions. Where Fokine, following in the footsteps of Noverre, wanted to make the ballet an imitation of life, Tudor has turned it rather into an interpretation of life, probing below the surface of action into the psychological workings which lie at the bottom of it. In this he has much in common with the purposes, if not with the methods, of the modern dancers.

He requires the strictest of academic technique as the dancer's foundation, but in his compositions he distorts it at every turn to produce the total result he is after. He has used to the full the psychological effect of curious and involved acrobatic lifts, and his invention is rich and intuitive throughout the whole range of movement. He works slowly, is an out-and-out perfectionist and makes the most stringent demands upon his dancers, both technically and emotionally.

Musically he is extraordinarily sensitive, not only to the outward form (against which he habitu-

Left: Annabelle Lyon and Hugh Laing in the Ballet Theatre revival of Anthony Tudor's "Jardin aux Lilas," first produced for the Ballet Club, London, in 1936. Right: Antony Tudor and Karen Conrad in "Jardin aux Lilas."

Right: Scene from Tudor's "Goyescas" (1941). Below: Agnes de Mille, Lucia Chase and Maria Karnilova in the Ballet Theatre revival of Tudor's "Judgment of Paris," originally produced for the London Ballet (1938).

Left: Hugh Laing and Nora Kaye in Tudor's "Pillar of Fire" Right: Annabelle Lyon, Lucia Chase and Nora Kaye in "Pillar of Fire" (1940).

ally composes phrases of movement in counterpoint rather than in rhythmic unison), but also to the inward spirit, which he never violates in the smallest degree. It is characteristic of his selection of music for his ballets that he manages to find works whose musical entity will not be strong enough to overbalance a choreographic setting. If it is not always music of the top rank as a result, it is nevertheless of suitable quality to make for unity in a total theatre work. That, manifestly, is of greater importance.

He makes no compromises with audiences and their possible likes and dislikes. He can be exceedingly cruel in mood, as in the tortured "Undertow," and he is not gentle in his caricature, as in the relentlessly sordid humors of "Judgment of Paris" and the pointed laughter at temperamental ballerinas in "Gala Performance." The sombreness of "Dark Elegies," set to the "Kindertotenlieder" of Mahler, is unrelieved, and he spares nothing of the emotional ordeal of the introverted heroine of "Pillar of Fire." There is naturally a section of the public that finds him too strong for pleasure, and the arch-classicists are not numbered among his admirers, but the great majority of ballet-goers recognize his genius and flock to his productions, no matter how "difficult" they may be.

It was at the instigation of Agnes de Mille, with whom he had worked in London, that he was

Left: Alicia Markova and Hugh Laing in Tudor's "Romeo and Juliet" (1943). Right: Antony Tudor and Nora Kaye in Tudor's "Dim Lustre" (1944).

invited by Richard Pleasant to come to this country in 1939 to participate as both dancer and choreographer in the Ballet Theatre project then being formed in New York. To the repertory of that company he contributed four works originally created for various London companies: "Jardin aux Lilas," "Judgment of Paris," "Gala Performance" and "Dark Elegies." To them he has since added five new works created in this country. (He is now at work on his sixth—based on a scenario taken from Proust with music by Gian-Carlo Menotti.)

One of these was the not very important assignment of making a ballet out of Granados's "Goyescas," which had already been unsuccessfully attempted by another choreographer. It was workmanlike but shortlived.

In 1942 he presented for the first time "Pillar of Fire," set to Schoenberg's "Verklaerte Nacht," which is generally considered to be his greatest work thus far and which won immediate acclaim. It dealt, probably for the first time in the ballet's history, with sex as a psychological instead of a purely romantic subject, and may properly be considered as inaugurating a new era for the ballet as a medium for the expression of profound and penetrating insight into human experience.

It served also to reveal Nora Kaye, for whom its central role was created, as one of the greatest of actress-dancers. Miss Kaye had already danced with marked success the romantic heroine of "Jar-

Left: Nana Gollner and Hugh Laing in Tudor's "Undertow" (1945). Right: Rosella Hightower in "Dim Lustre."

din aux Lilas," and the broadly satirized Russian ballerina in "Gala Performance." She was still to be seen in the witty, high comedy of his later "Dim Lustre," and to follow Markova as Juliet in his version of "Romeo and Juliet." Though she has exhibited her notable gifts in the works of other choreographers as well as in many traditional classic roles, it was under Tudor's guidance that she assumed her place among the outstanding artists of the contemporary ballet.

"Romeo and Juliet" was created for Alicia Markova and provided her with one of her finest roles. It gave her an opportunity to prove herself to be not only the mistress of the classic style which so many of her other roles had proclaimed her, but also an actress of top rank. In all his ballets, Tudor has been extraordinarily successful in bringing out qualities in individual dancers which perhaps they themselves have not been aware of, and which the conventional repertoire would be unlikely to discover. Two cases in point are the violently dramatic roles for which he cast with supreme success two predominantly classic ballerinas, Nana Gollner and Alicia Alonso, in "Undertow."

In this last-named work, Tudor carried his delving into the recesses of the human mentality to new depths; so much so, indeed, that he required a kind of psychoanalytical symbolism for his full expression. If this is a grim, somewhat obscure and unpleasant work, it is also a courageous and disturbing one. Here for the first time, incidentally, he employed music especially composed for the purpose instead of relying on already existing compositions. It was written by William Schuman.

Of all his dancers, Hugh Laing has been the most indispensable. Having worked with him in England and collaborated with him on the founding of the London Ballet Company in 1938, he also came to America with him and has danced the leading male roles in all his ballets here. Laing's dramatic powers are broad, intensely keyed and sensitive; he can project the truth of the pitiful victim of "Undertow," the romantic lover of "Jardin aux Lilas," the despicable voluptuary of "Pillar of Fire," the impetuous Romeo, and the sinister waiter in "Judgment of Paris" with equal style and conviction. Among the male dancers of the ballet he is in a class apart.

As for Tudor himself, if Balanchine is hailed as the leader of the neo-classic field, dealing in purely formal aesthetics, he is equally the leader of the neo-romantic, in which the aesthetic includes primarily expressive and psychological values.

AMERICAN ROOTS

The founding of the Ballet Theatre was an important step in the development of the ballet in America; potentially, indeed, the most important step that has been taken, except for Lincoln Kirstein's long-term coordination of teaching and producing. The basic approach of its founder, Richard Pleasant, was altogether different from Kirstein's, though in no sense competitive with it. Instead of wishing to plant seed for the ultimate emergence of a ballet which should be American in character, it was his purpose to establish a producing organization which in its own field should be the equivalent of a museum of art. In it he wanted to give a place to already existing works representative of all periods and national origins, while simultaneously sponsoring the creation of new works from all contemporary sources. His initial set-up included a classical wing, a Fokine-Diaghileff-Russian wing, and contemporary American, British, Negro and Spanish wings. It was his

Left: Agnes de Mille and Warren Leonard in "May Day" (1929). Center: Agnes de Mille in her solo, "Civil War" (1929). Right: Agnes de Mille in her solo, "Ballet Class" (1928).

Above: Scene from de Mille's ballet, "Three Virgins and a Devil," produced by Ballet Theatre (1941). Left: Scene from de Mille's "Drums Sound in Hackensack," the first ballet to be created by any one but Kurt Jooss for the Jooss Ballet (1941).

Left: Agnes de Mille and Frederic Franklin in "Rodeo," produced for the Ballet Russe de Monte Carlo (1942).
Right: Jerome Robbins in "Three Virgins and a Devil," a brief role in which he made his first success.

Left: Anton Dolin and Janet Reed in de Mille's "Tally-Ho!" (1944). Right: Paul Haakon and Philip Gordon in de Mille's "Hero Ballet" in the revue "Hooray for What?" (1937).

intention ultimately to enlarge his definition of ballet to include also productions by the American modern dancers. The preparations for the initial season were long and financially as expensive as such an enterprise must necessarily be if it is to be worthy of its ideals, and the project was not taken too seriously by the cynics in advance. To their great surprise, however, it established itself as a success, both artistically and popularly, overnight.

Unfortunately, intrigues within and without the organization undermined its foundations very shortly on the heels of success, Pleasant's policy was repudiated and he was forced to resign. The company was refashioned to conform as nearly as possible to the general pattern of the Ballet Russe, and even billed its repertoire as "Russian Ballet." Only the persistence of some of the personnel and the solid foundations laid in its beginnings kept it from disappearing as a major organization. Through all its vicissitudes and vacillations in policy, however, it has managed to maintain a company of unusually high standing and to sponsor the work of several new choreographers of ability. Recently it has undergone another internal reorganization, and what its future will be only time will tell.

In its initial season in 1940 it introduced Tudor to American audiences, presented the first ballet by Agnes de Mille (a work for Negro dancers called "Black Ritual," now out of the repertoire) and made a notable experiment, though an unsuccessful one at the box-office, in combining speech with ballet. This was "The Great American Goof," for which William Saroyan wrote the book and Eugene Loring designed the choreography.

Miss de Mille also produced her "Three Virgins and a Devil" and the more recent "Tally-Ho!" for this company, though her most successful ballet, "Rodeo," and her most American one in subject, interestingly enough, was sponsored by the Ballet Russe de Monte Carlo.

De Mille's "Civil War Ballet" in the musical comedy, "Bloomer Girl" (1944).

The de Mille ballet, "Forty Minutes for Lunch," in the musical comedy, "One Touch of Venus" (1944). Sono Osato, Mary Martin and Peter Birch at right.

Viola Essen and Eugene Loring in Adolph Bolm's "Peter and the Wolf," produced by Ballet Theatre (1940).

Left: Miriam Golden and Eugene Loring in Loring's "The Great American Goof," produced by Ballet Theatre (1940). Center: Patricia Bowman in Mikhail Mordkin's "Voices of Spring" (1939). Right: Nana Gollner in "Swan Lake."

Jerome Robbins made his highly distinguished debut as a choreographer with the fresh and original "Fancy Free" in the later repertory of the Ballet Theatre, to be followed by his quite different "Interplay" and "Facsimile". Michael Kidd has made an equally distinguished bow as a choreographer with the same company, presenting the, again, altogether original "On Stage!"

It is clear that, whatever the particular philosophy and the particular sources may be, a distinctively American school of ballet is emerging. No doubt some of this is due to the fact that during the war years the influence of Europe has been less than formerly. But considerable specific groundwork has been laid by many individuals over the years. Adolph Bolm, Fokine, Mikhail Mordkin, Alexander Gavrilov, and other Russians all started American ballets at one time or another which lasted for longer or shorter periods. Of recent years there have been significant movements under the direction of native-born artists.

Scene from Ballet Theatre's revival of Loring's "Billy the Kid," originally produced by the Ballet Caravan in 1939.

Left: Michael Kidd and Janet Reed in Kidd's first ballet, "On Stage!", produced by Ballet Theatre (1945). Right: John Kriza and Nora Kaye in "On Stage!". Below: Jerome Robbins in his own "Fancy Free," produced by Ballet Theatre (1944).

Ruth Page has done yeoman work in the Chicago Opera, in the late Federal Theatre, and in such private enterprises as the Page-Stone Ballet, in which her associate and collaborator was Bentley Stone. Out of this collaboration has come one of the best and most characteristic of American ballets, "Frankie and Johnny," originally produced for the Federal Theatre and later absorbed into the repertory of the Ballet. Russe de Monte Carlo.

In Philadelphia, Catherine Littlefield did admirable spade work with her Philadelphia Ballet and later carried her activities briefly to the Chicago Opera. "Barn Dance," now in the repertory of the Ballet Theatre, "Café Society," "Terminal" and "Ladies' Better Dresses" were typically American genre pieces which found a place in her repertoire alongside works in the classic vein. From her company have come any

Above: Annabelle Lyon in "Pas de Quatre." Nana Gollner in the first act of "Giselle." Alicia Alonso in "Les Sylphides." Karen Conrad in the "Blue Bird" variation from "The Sleeping Beauty."

Below: Alicia Alonso in "Princess Aurora." Sono Osato in David Lichine's "Prodigal Son." Rosella Hightower in "Pas de Quatre." Nora Kaye.

Above left: Ruth Page and Bentley Stone. Right: John Kriza and Alicia Markova in Anton Dolin's "The Romantic Age" (1942).

Above: Ruthanna Boris. Below: Paul Haakon.

number of important young dancers such as Karen Conrad and Joan McCracken.

Lincoln Kirstein's small company called Ballet Caravan, an offshoot of his larger American Ballet project, sponsored a number of ballets by young native choreographers, and discovered one of the richest talents in this field in Eugene Loring. His "Billy the Kid," now in the repertory of the Ballet Theatre, has already become something of a modern classic. Also for the Caravan he produced "City Portrait" and "Yankee Clipper," both interesting works. Lew Christensen, another Caravan discovery, contributed "Filling Station," "Charade," and several other works to the repertoire, and from William Dollar came "Promenade," "Juke Box," "Air and Variations," "Constantia" and others.

Out of the American Ballet and its subsidiary companies and its school have come any number of leading dancers now active in other companies. Among them are Alicia Alonso, one of the truly great classic ballerinas and the logical successor to that other Alicia, Markova, who is today the supreme exemplar of the classic art; Nora Kaye and Michael Kidd, mainstays of

Janet Reed.

Above left: Ruth Page as Frankie in "Frankie and Johnny," created by her and Bentley Stone for the Federal Theatre, Chicago (1938). Right: Bentley Stone as Johnny in "Frankie and Johnny."

Left: Catherine Littlefield and Thomas Cannon in Littlefield's version of "Daphnis and Chloe," produced for the Philadelphia Ballet (1937). Right: Adolph Bolm in "Apollo Musagetes," as produced by him at the Library of Congress, Washington (1928).

Above left: Scene from Eugene Loring's "Harlequin for President," presented by the Ballet Caravan (1936). Above right: Eugene Loring and Marie-Jeanne in Loring's "Billy the Kid," as presented by the Ballet Caravan (1939). Lower right: Dorothie Littlefield and Thomas Cannon in Catherine Littlefield's "Barn Dance," produced by the Philadelphia Ballet (1937).

the Ballet Theatre; Ruthanna Boris, one of the brighest lights of the Ballet Russe de Monte Carlo; Marie-Jeanne, Mary Ellen Moylan, and the rising young choreographer, Todd Bolender, who have all contributed to this latter company.

In San Francisco the ballet of the opera company has had a vigorous life of its own, especially under the direction of William Christensen. Out of its ranks have come some excellent dancers, including at the head of the list the delightful Janet Reed, one of the bright particular stars of the Ballet Theatre.

It is too early to prophesy where all this creative activity is leading, but it would seem to have taken a direction of its own and to possess undeniable vitality. It would be a mistake to assume that the mere making of ballets on American themes constitutes the basis of an American ballet. It is true that most of the works thus far created in this country have been

Right: William Dollar. Below: Scene from the Page-Stone ballet, "Guns and Castanets," produced for the Federal Theatre, Chicago (1938). Opposite page, top: Scene from William Dollar's "Promenade," presented by the Ballet Caravan (1936). Bottom: Scene from Lew Christensen's "Filling Station," produced by the Ballet Caravan (1938).

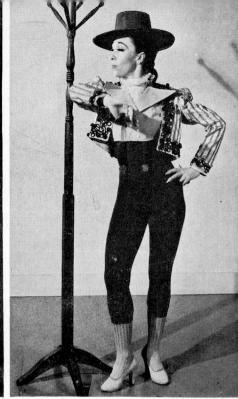

Carmelita Maracci, who combines classic Spanish dance and ballet in a unique and pungent modern style of her own.

on American themes, but their creative quality lies deeper than that. Leonide Massine once created a ballet on an American theme called "Union Pacific," but it was far less American in quality than Agnes de Mille's "Three Virgins and a Devil," for example, which has a medieval theme, Italian music, and English scenario, scenery and costumes. It is the American mind that constitutes the native element, and this manifests itself not only in the choice of subject, but also in the method of composition and more particularly in the approach to movement itself.

Naturally, the so-called modern dance has had considerable influence in these latter departments. It is a native American development to begin with and its persuasiveness has been considerable among the younger dancers in the local ballet field. In addition, it has also been a factor in the ballet as a whole ever since the paths of the two arts crossed at the time of the emergence of Fokine in the wake of Isadora. The frequent indications of this influence in important works since the beginning of the modern ballet have already been noted in passing.

PART FOUR

Dance as a Means of Communication

INDUBITABLY no other art form has been so inaptly named as the "modern dance." Not only is the phrase non-descriptive, but it is markedly inaccurate, since there is absolutely nothing modern about modern dance. It is, as a matter of fact, virtually basic dance, the oldest of all dance forms. The modern dancer, instead of employing the cumulative resources of academic tradition, cuts through directly to the source of all dancing. He utilizes the principle that every emotional state tends to express itself in movement, and that the movements thus created spontaneously, though they are not representational, reflect accurately in each case the character of the particular emotional state. Because of the inherent contagion of bodily movement, which makes the onlooker feel sympathetically in his own musculature the exertions he sees in somebody else's musculature, the dancer is able to convey through movement the most intangible emotional experience. This is the prime purpose of the modern dance; it is not interested in spectacle, but in the communication of emotional experiences—intuitive perceptions, elusive truths—which cannot be communicated in reasoned terms or reduced to mere statement of fact.

This principle is at least as old as man himself; primitive societies, as we have seen, have found it so potent that they have called it magic and based religious and social practices on it. But it had never been consciously utilized as the basis of art, so far as any record exists, until the turn of the present century when Isadora Duncan made it the very center and source of her practices, and the so-called modern dance was born.

Isadora Duncan.

Opposite page: Isadora Duncan in "La Marseillaise."

ISADORA DUNCAN

Isadora discovered it for herself through experience and not by studying any previous systems, past or present. She has recorded her theories and her struggles toward the achievement of them in her autobiography and in the post-humous collection of her writings called "The Art of the Dance," which is one of the master works of dance literature. She tells with wonderful clarity of her conviction that all expressive movement sprang from the "soul," by which she meant the seat of the emotions; of how she stood for hours before the mirror trying to locate the actual place in the body where these impulses centered; of how she evolved, under certain emotional stimulation, key movements which were so true and so fundamental that they gave rise auto-matically to other related movements growing out of them and developing the same theme. It was her deepest desire to discard all artifices, all invention, all traditional methods and established vocabularies of movement such as the ballet employed, and to get to the natural source of man's expressiveness, using only the natural movements of the body without acrobatic exaggeration or surface ornamentation, and allowing them to produce themselves only under inner compulsion.

There was nothing at all of the theatre in her dancing. It was a purely lyric art; that is, one of personal expression rather than of characterization, storytelling or the exhibition of skills. Her performances were therefore not theatrical presentations but dance recitals, an altogether new form for the art.

Her chief inspiration came from music; in Chopin, Tchaikovsky, Wagner, Beethoven, Gluck, she found, in a sense, a model for her practice. Here was an expression of inner feeling such as she sought, and though it was considered heresy to dance to such music she could not help herself. Contrary to popular opinion both of her own time and later, she made no effort whatever to "in-terpret" the music or to "visualize" it; it served simply as the "motor" which she placed in her "soul" to make it function. She acknowledged that this was not an ideal practice, and she inferred that some day when she had fully mastered the art of producing movement she would dispense with it, but that day never came.

Quite in keeping with her whole desire for affirming nature and denying artifice, she turned her back completely on the conventional methods of dance costuming with their restrictive corsets and

shoes and their general fanciness and ostentation. To the horror of the world, she took off not only her corsets but also her shoes and stockings and danced barefooted and barelegged in the simplest of Greek tunics. Here the body was free to move, free to reveal itself in the full beauty of what it actually was without pretense or convention.

For one long period she turned to ancient Greece as her guide, studied the dancing figures in the museums, and at last actually went to Greece. But in the end she concluded that she was not a Greek, even at heart, but primarily a Scotch-Irish-American. There was more than just fantasy, however, in her feeling of kinship with ancient Greece, for though nobody today can say authoritatively how the Greeks danced, it seems likely that their great choric dramas were built on principles of movement very similar to Isadora's rediscovery of basic dance.

It is not surprising that the America of President McKinley's day rejected Isadora's art, for all that no other country and no other time could possibly have mothered it. New forces were at work in the world's thinking, and painters, musicians, architects, psychologists, folklorists, actors, physiologists, philosophers, everywhere were turning with fresh interest to the relations which existed between the inner, emotional man and his outward means of expression. In Russia, as has already been noted, Fokine was reacting with marked sensitiveness in his own field of the dance, reforming a tradition so old and so deep-seated that it could never be wholly denied. In America no such tradition existed; when the impetus of the dawning new world mentality touched the dance here there were no such resistances to be met within the art itself. Isadora went directly to the roots of the subject, where Fokine inevitably only pruned out the dead wood and allowed new growth to function on the old plant.

It is significant, also, that though Isadora was received with acclaim (as well as with an admixture of shocked dismay) all over Europe, it was in Germany, where the French-Italian classic tradition had never taken firm root, that she was most fully understood. That she was persecuted there, too, goes without saying, for she was flying in the face of worldwide traditions other than those of the dance, in her daring costume, for use of music, her theories of education and of personal morality. Nevertheless, it was there that her ideas took hold most firmly and, a full generation after she had left the country, resulted in the emergence of the vital modern dance movement of the German Republic after World War I.

Meanwhile in her native land other influences were at work. That she was responsible for them in a measure cannot be gainsaid, for even a world that rejected her art with self-righteous indignation could not resist the effects of its general upheaval. "Barefoot" dancers were all about, "natural" dancers abounded, practically everybody "interpreted" the musical classics, and more "Greeks" flitted about the dance world than had ever done so before even in the peak days of the Renaissance. It is ironic, however, that in America where the modern dance has developed to its fullest expression, it can trace no direct line of descent from Isadora. Her own pupils who came to this country in later years, and their pupils in turn (with such notable exceptions as Anita Zahn, Kathleen Hinni and Julia Levien) have attempted to carry on in her original vein of forty or fifty years ago, making it almost as traditional in its own way as the ballet itself, instead of applying her essential principles of basic dance to the everchanging contemporary emotional and cultural situation and allowing outward forms to be shaped by the times.

sentation in a "smoking concert" on the New York Theatre Roof. It won a sensational artistic success, however, in Europe and later in this country, and was the beginning of a tremendous upsurge of imitative "Oriental" dancing. Her own dancing made no pretense to being authentic in style; it was merely a pictorial approximation of Eastern styles, used for its spectacular qualities together with its aspects of religious ritual.

St. Denis was never concerned with technical method, but relied on a native gift for beautiful movement, a facility for improvisation and an instinct for theatrical effect. When, however, she married her young dancing partner, Ted Shawn, and their Denishawn school and company came into being, other elements were added. Shawn, formerly a divinity student, shared St. Denis's approach to religious values in the dance. He was also as predominantly theatrical in taste as she was. But his interests were much broader, his outlook more eclectic and his respect for technical training considerably more marked. Though the Denishawn method still contained much Oriental material, it also dealt with Spanish and American Indian material, and employed a basic technique adapted to barefoot use from the academic ballet. In its later years it embraced many other methods, including Dalcroze Eurythmics and even the modern German dance.

As an advocate of nudity, Shawn surpassed Isadora herself. Obviously, the body as the expressive instrument of the dance should be allowed all freedom. He was also a militant worker for the return of men to dancing, and for the destruction of the stigma of effeminacy which had clung to the male dancer ever since his decline as an institution in the nineteenth century ballet.

In such an atmosphere St. Denis could not well have remained exclusively in her earlier Oriental pattern, even if she had been so inclined. Perhaps her most important innovation during these years

A group of Denishawn dancers (Doris Humphrey, center) after their tour of the Orient in the mid-1920's.

Ted Shawn and the Denishawn company in the Indian dance-drama, "Thunderbird," in the 1920's.

was her idea of "music visualization." This was frankly influenced by Isadora's use of concert music, but it added a practice instituted by Emile Jaques-Dalcroze in his system of musical education whereby the form of a symphonic work was mirrored by having each dancer follow a specific instrument in a symphonic score note for note, under the overall direction of a choreographer. In this new orchestral approach to dancing, St. Denis had the assistance of one of her young dancers, Doris Humphrey, who was largely responsible for freeing the form from its implicit rigidity and developing it into a mature and legitimate practice. St. Denis has claimed in her autobiography that this was the beginning of what grew later into the American modern dance, and it is a claim that would be hard to deny.

The modern dance, however, was not so much an outgrowth of Denishawn as a rebellion against it. New ideas among its dancers, inspired by progress in outside fields, were frowned upon officially, and important defections occurred in its ranks. First Martha Graham left, then Doris Humphrey and Charles Weidman, to build independently upon their own artistic convictions. Ultimately Denishawn itself was dissolved, with St. Denis devoting herself to the religious dance and Shawn first organizing a men's group and later establishing a "university of the dance" at Jacob's Pillow, near Lee, Mass. The old organization had served its purpose nobly. A new era in the dance was coming into being—the most prolific, the most richly creative, the most widespread era the dance has ever enjoyed in America.

Left: Ted Shawn in his Spanish suite. Right: Barton Mumaw, principal dancer of Shawn's men's group, in the "Dayak Spear Dance."

MARY WIGMAN

But meanwhile there were important activities in Europe. The seed planted by Isadora was bearing fruit. Immediately in her wake there had been a wealth of fresh accomplishment, especially in Germany and Austria. It was not so much an imitation of her as it was a freeing of native impulses under the stimulation of her example. It ranged all the way from the educational systems of Bode and Dalcroze to the performances of such widely popular lyric artists as the Wiesenthal Sisters, Clothilde von Derp, and Ronny Johansson.

At the close of the war, however, there were new and more profound manifestations of the same fundamental impulses. Not only were the German people as a whole encouraged to use the dance as a physical means to rehabilitate themselves after their years of wartime undernourishment, but a phenomenal interest arose in the dance as an expressive art.

Among the many artists of greater or lesser achievement, was one who towered above the scene like a giant. Except for Isadora herself, no figure in the history of the modern dance occupies a higher position than Mary Wigman, in part for her specific artistic creations, but mainly for her widening of the range and advancement of the underlying theory of the art. She had studied with Dalcroze at Hellerau, and had spent the war years as a pupil of Rudolf von Laban in Switzerland. The Dalcroze Institute had been not only an extremely advanced institution for musical education, in which music was related directly to movement, but had also expanded naturally into modern theatre experimentation along the lines of Adolphe Appia and Gordon Craig and their colleagues, and was one of the most stimulating artistic centers in Europe. Laban was virtually the father of the theory of the German modern dance, having experimented in the psychology of movement, the analysis of space, and many other problems. From both these sources she was undoubtedly enriched, but when she broke away at last to work independently, it was along quite different lines.

Her dance, like Isadora's, grew out of "ecstasy," but where Isadora allowed her ecstasy to flow along the course of the music that inspired it, Wigman demanded that her ecstasy create its own formal expression. Form, indeed, was for her as indispensable a part of the creative process as emotional impulse.

In many of her early dances, in order to free herself from the domination of musical form, from which Isadora had never been able to escape, she composed works entirely without music, and great portions of her repertoire continued to be either entirely musicless or to employ musicless passages. Once this pressing problem of absolute choreographic form was solved, she made free use of music, and in this lay one of her most valuable contributions, for it marked a return to the practice of basic dance. Her characteristic method was to use a simple melodic line, frequently played on a primitive flute or something of the sort, with rhythmic support by percussion instruments of many kinds. Thus, like primitive dancers, she projected her own song and her own pulse into the music that accompanied her. Tendencies in this direction were general, it is true, throughout the German field, but Wigman achieved by far the most impressive results with them. It is possible to believe, indeed,

Opposite page: Mary Wigman in "Tanz des Kleides" (1930).

Left: Mary Wigman in "Zweispiele" (1939). Right: Mary Wigman in "Tanz der Dunklen Königin" (1939).

that in her application of first principles of basic dance, she has shown the way to the perfect solution of the problem of music's relation to dance. That a special type of musician, highly sensitive to movement and willing to sacrifice traditional musical theories, is required, goes without saying, but the difficulties involved in practice do not in any degree invalidate the soundness of the principle.

Another major contribution of Wigman was her awareness of space. Isadora moved as a sculptural figure, as it were, self-contained and complete, regardless of physical surroundings; Wigman, on the other hand, placed her dance consciously in a three-dimensional area, relating the moving figure always to its surroundings in what might be called an architectural sense. Laban's experiments with space had been largely intellectual; he had seen the human body as standing theoretically in the center of a many-sided geometrical figure, and had formulated the directions and the extents and the paths of travel in which its various members could move. Wigman's attitude to the subject was emotional; she felt space as the medium through which she moved in much the same way as the swimmer feels water. Where Isadora's dance was merely a lyric outpouring of personal emotion, to all intents and purposes in a vacuum, Wigman's became inherently dramatic because of this constant awareness of space as an element presenting limitations to the range of movement or resistance to actual motor effort, and in general as a symbolic representation of the universe in which the single individual finds himself.

If Isadora freed the dance from the exclusive use of an established vocabulary of specific movements and sought to establish a definite link between inner feeling and outward gesture, her results

"Totentanz" by Mary Wigman (1926).

were of a fairly general nature. A child of her own period, she was strongly influenced by its standards. For her a work of art must be "beautiful," and the aesthetic of the Pre-Raphaelite Brotherhood
came perhaps nearest to conditioning her concept of beauty. She also had her generation's attitude
toward Greek art as being the epitome of simple, always harmonious line and form, even though the
subject might be inharmonious and tragic. In her writings, and necessarily in her thinking as well,
she spelled Love, Truth, Beauty, Life, and all such generic terms, with capital letters. It was entirely
logical, then, that the movements she evolved should be limited in range, natural in quality (so long
as the more realistic and inharmonious aspects of nature were excluded), and should consist chiefly
of such fundamental and elementary ingredients as running and skipping. Since her power of pro-
jecting emotion was incredibly great, this was all the means she required.

Wigman, however, also a child of her age, was less bound to abstract standards of beauty. Her
movement was conceived in the inner recesses of her individual psychology, and she had trained her
body to serve as a transparency through which she could express the subtlest of emotional shadings.
No movements, however odd or superficially ugly, were rejected so long as they were evocative.
Her entire body was a sensitive instrument, and the movement it produced was never invented but
always intuitively realized, whether noble in style or grotesque.

Thus, if Isadora discovered the "soul" of the dance, Wigman gave it its body. There is much
about her work that is alien to American taste; her costuming is curiously unattractive, her philosophical bent, her preoccupation with death, her general introspectiveness, are all essentially Ger-

man and demand to be seen as such before they can be accepted. But this is merely a process of translation such as any foreign art must undergo. Her greatness can never be denied, and her three American tours had a broadening and salutary influence on the American dance.

Happily in World War II there was no tendency in America as there was in World War I to ban all German art in an excess of nationalism. Beethoven and Brahms and Bach were recognized as transcending nationality, and even Wagner's operas, so beloved of Hitler, were kept in the repertories of our opera houses and in their original tongue. It would be similarly unthinkable to ignore or underestimate the greatness of Wigman on grounds of nationality. German she certainly is, but she was never remotely sympathetic to the Nazi regime; she was spied upon by "party" members of her own staff, and eventually uprooted from her school and disfranchised through their efforts. At the close of the war she was found in Leipzig, living in poverty, and her teaching was resumed there on an extremely modest private basis pending the reopening of the Leipzig Musikhochschule.

HANYA HOLM

Many of her principles were naturalized in this country through Hanya Holm, who was a member of the original dance group with which Wigman made history in Europe in the early '20's, later headed the faculty of the central Wigman school in Dresden, and finally came to New York during Wigman's tours of this country to open a branch of her school.

Holm had not been in this country for many months before she had fallen completely in love with its vigorous rhythm of living, the fresh vitality of its young dancers, its speed and dash, and she realized that the future lay here for her and her ideas of the dance. Its rhythms, too, must be more vigorous, and she began a process of quite intuitive adaptation to the new land and its pulse. Over the intervening years she has evolved a personal art and a personal method, which, though rooted in Wigman's theory, are so clearly of American influence and American growth as to be essentially a native product. Indeed, when one speaks of American modern dance, one includes Hanya Holm as a matter of indisputable course; her dance, like herself, has long since become an American citizen.

Partly because of her gifts as an educator and partly because she is possessed of so sound a system of education, she has necessarily spent most of her energies in teaching. She has nevertheless created a number of choreographic works of decided individuality. Shortly before she came to this country, she collaborated with Wigman on the production of a massive anti-war work called "Totenmal," presented in Munich in 1930. This highly experimental theatre piece involved a huge company of dancers, a speech-chorus and a large percussion orchestra. But she was in this country for six full years before she felt she was ready to present a composition which had grown out of her new environment. When she did, it was a significant one. Created for the Bennington Festival in 1937, it was called "Trend." It employed a large group and soloists (of whom Holm was one, but by no means in a stellar sense), and its music included the extremely radical all-percussion "Ionization" of

Hanya Holm in a dance study.

Hanya Holm in "Trend" (1937).

Edgar Varèse. Though Holm's style had seemed essentially lyric, this proved to be an intensely dramatic work and one which made use of all the elements of the theatre, including the first truly modern stage setting the American dance had seen. It was designed by Arch Lauterer. It was clear at once that here was an important choreographer.

Other and smaller works created for subsequent Bennington Festivals were "Dance of Work and Play" and "Dance Sonata." Since the end of these festivals at the beginning of World War II, Holm has produced new works each summer for the festival at the Fine Arts Center in Colorado Springs. Among these works are "From This Earth," "Namesake," "Orestes and the Furies," "What So Proudly We Hail," and most recently, "What Dreams May Come," "Walt Whitman Suite" and "Windows."

Her compositions, whether dramatic, humorous or lyric, are characterized by an instinctive sense of form, a fine musicianship (she was also a graduate of the Dalcroze Institute at Hellerau), and a lively interest in experimentation. "The Golden Fleece," for example, was an attempt to choreograph a surrealist theme and costumes by Kurt Seligmann, and though it was not successful, it was distinctly courageous. Her works are almost invariably of musical interest, and such modern American composers as Roy Harris, Harrison Kerr, Norman Lloyd, John Cage, and Gregory Tucker have provided her with scores.

The great period of the modern American dance—actually the beginning of its second generation —can be said to have started in the mid-1920's. Martha Graham gave her first independent New York recital in 1926; 1927 saw the debut of Helen Tamiris; early in 1928 Doris Humphrey and Charles Weidman set out on their own, assisted by a group from Denishawn, with which institution they were still connected.

Dance recitals of one sort and another had already become numerous, but they were in the main either evidences of artistic tendencies definitely on the decline or else merely performances by individuals of certain personal gifts but no particular direction. What was shaping itself as the modern dance had no definable quality that separated it from these other activities, yet there was from the beginning a sense of latent vitality in it that set it somehow apart.

In retrospect it is now possible to see the general trend of the whole period; the dance was transforming itself from an imitative art into a creative one. The dancer, having been touched by Isadora's

Scene from Holm's first production of "Trend" at the Bennington Festival of 1937.

Scene from Holm's "Orestes and the Furies" (1943).

Hanya Holm and Jerome Andrews in "What Dreams May Come" (1944).

revelation of the expression of inner personal experience, was rebelling against merely pretending theatrically to be somebody else, whether a Hindu goddess, an Aztec warrior, a butterfly or a swan, and mimicking that somebody's behavior. The first problem was to throw off all these "false whiskers," so to speak, and get to the heart of one's own emotional self according to Isadora's example.

But Isadora's dance was not of the theatre, as she had freely admitted. The second problem, accordingly, was to develop this great discovery of "self-expression" in the dance back into an art of the theatre. Music was the instrument for solving the first problem; one simply let the music stir the emotions into action as Isadora had done. The next step was to get rid of this self-inflicted tyranny of music, as Wigman had done, so that expressive movement could be free to create its own forms. When movement had thus been isolated so that it could function without leaning either on musical form or theatrical impersonation, the actual substance of the dance had been found. From that point on the dancer was really in the position of an artist who knew his materials. Little by little he was able to add music where he needed it, costumes and scenery, characterization and dramatic situation, even spoken words, and still keep movement as the stuff of his art with his own emotional convictions as its animator.

DORIS HUMPHREY

Of all the dancers of this notable second generation, Doris Humphrey best exemplifies this line of development. In her early work with St. Denis on "music visualizations" she had begun to approach the subject of non-representational movement. At this stage it was still formally the slave of music, but by 1924 she had created a choreographic "visualization" of Edward MacDowell's "Sonata Tragica" which had so much independent form that the music was finally discarded and it was performed in silence. But no firm basis for creating in terms of absolute dance had been laid by this procedure, for music had been its shaping force whether it was audibly played or not. Two other works carried these experiments to fulfillment. One was "Water Study," which Humphrey knew was a transitional step, for it was merely substituting external nature rhythms for the rhythms of music as a formal guide. (Actually its value lay not in its recourse to an outward model but rather in its technical employment of the rhythms of breath and blood pulse as a basis for group movement.) The second work was "Drama of Motion," a three-part group composition without music, which depended on no auxiliary devices whatever, and was a work of pure dance as absolute as any symphony.

In the six years that had elapsed between the "Tragica" and "Drama of Motion," Humphrey had evolved an extraordinarily original and thoroughly sound theory. She was not at the moment concerned with the relation of emotional impulse to movement; that was a creative matter with which she knew how to deal. What she was seeking was rather the nature of motion in space, irrespective of how it was inspired, so that she might find principles on which to build in terms of independent

Doris Humphrey in her solo, "Circular Descent" (1931). Opposite page: Doris Humphrey in "New Dance" (1935).

form. Like Isadora, she stood for hours before the mirror, but unlike Isadora, she was not seeking any mystical enlightenment; she was watching the actual mass of her body in its relation to gravity and the behavior patterns that emerged from this relationship. Her findings, based not only on observation but also on knowledge of the body and the principles of physics involved, constitute one of the most important contributions that anybody has made to dance theory. It actually comprises what might be called the kinetic laws of the dance.

The matter of equilibrium was the crux of her experimentation. She knew that the body tends to be thrown off balance by any movement, however slight, and that it is constantly making automatic compensatory motions to maintain equilibrium. In her experiments before the mirror she studied the effects of a sideward swaying that increased in range until it actually involved falling to the ground. The wider the sway and the greater the resulting loss of equilibrium, the more vigorous the compensatory movements that were automatically made to restore balance. Also, the speed with which the body fell increased as the fall progressed. All motion, then, she concluded, was "an arc between two deaths"; there was the "death" of complete inactivity in which there was no contest with gravity, and at the other extreme was the "death" of destruction in which gravity had defeated all efforts at resistance.

Obviously, the movements that were most interesting to watch were those in the sphere of danger, where destruction was constantly being defied and at the crucial moment avoided. As Wigman had made space her dramatic antagonist, Humphrey thus made gravity hers, and gave her dance immediately a color of drama in its very essence. The fundamental rhythm of moving now appeared clear-

ly to be the alternation between balance and unbalance, between fall and recovery; the natural increase in speed as the body approaches the bottom of its potential fall adds a dynamic element by invoking a corresponding increase in muscular tension to resist it. Other natural and basic principles of design are involved in the fact that compensatory motions are inevitably opposite in direction and at least equal in strength to the forces that are tending to produce the unbalance.

No more brilliant discovery has ever been made in the technical departments of the dance; it enunciates fundamental principles which, though supremely simple, affect the art in all its functional aspects. Its ramifications are so broad as actually to make possible the existence of movement as an absolute medium like music. Such rich creative possibilities were unfolded in this absolute field that Humphrey has continued to compose in its terms throughout her career, even after she had moved on to other developments, and some of her greatest works have been in this vein.

Having freed her basic movement from all its outside dependencies, however, she immediately began building toward large theatre forms. There were many compositions of high quality during this transition, containing experiments with various kinds of music outside the orthodox orchestral

Doris Humphrey and group in "Decade" (1938).

range, and with settings, costumes, speech. "Life of the Bee," with sound accompaniment but no music; "La Valse," to Ravel's music; "Orestes," to Milhaud's music for orchestra and chorus; "Dionysiaques," to music of Florent Schmitt, "The Shakers," using speech, accordion and voice, were notable examples.

But the full fruition of her genius as a choreographer and a master of large forms came with that period which was introduced by the "New Dance" trilogy, and which also includes "Passacaglia" and "Inquest" among its achievements. The trilogy, which consists of "Theatre Piece," "With My Red Fires" and "New Dance," is a heroic theatre work on the subject of man's relation to man, and it may well be, as many experienced dancegoers believe, the outstanding masterpiece of the American dance. Its first section is a protest against competition in terms of pungent satire; its second section is a tragedy of universal dimensions based on human possessiveness, with its principal figures personally characterized; its third section is a resolution of the preceding themes of conflict in terms of absolute dance.

Both this last section and "Passacaglia" are compositions of deep emotional significance and

Group passage from Humphrey's "New Dance."

dramatic content though without literary program. So sure was their creator's grasp of the medium that, though for "New Dance" a special musical score was composed by Wallingford Riegger, in "Passacaglia" she dared to match her choreographic concept against the formal mastery of Bach's C minor passacaglia without fear of its being overshadowed.

"Inquest" departs altogether in approach from everything that has gone before. It is a burning tragedy of social protest, using a spoken text out of Ruskin's "Sesame and Lilies" as well as an eloquent score by Norman Lloyd, and translating a sordid story by means of both pantomimic action and high abstraction into universal terms of moving beauty. This work, indeed, may prove to be the opening of still another period of artistic progression, for it manifestly touches new issues to life.

Humphrey has recently retired as a dancer (and also as a teacher, except for one master class in composition) in order to devote herself exclusively to choreography. Besides being a great artist and a great theorist, she is in this field unquestionably the most important figure who has yet arisen in the American dance.

CHARLES WEIDMAN

Charles Weidman has been closely associated with her ever since the Denishawn days, to their mutual advantage. Not only his personal presence in the company, but also his interest in developing male dancers in the so largely female-dominated modern dance, made it possible for the Humphrey-Weidman company to have both men and women in its casts from the very beginning. This was obviously a better balanced arrangement than that which generally prevailed as an inheritance from Isadora's exclusively feminine ensembles.

Weidman's dance is altogether distinctive and arises out of a very different basis from that of any of his colleagues. Though he has developed skills in absolute dance, for he is a broadly educated dancer, he works best and most significantly both as dancer and as choreographer in terms of movement that derives from pantomime. It is by no means realistic pantomime when he gets through with it, for he takes actual gesture and reduces it to its very essence as movement.

Sometimes it is dramatic, as in his group composition, "Lynch Town," which is both exciting and terrifying, and in the lurid melodrama of his "This Passion"; sometimes it is poignant, as in his bio-

Doris Humphrey and Charles Weidman in Humphrey's "Inquest" (1944).

Opposite page: Scene from the Federal Theatre (New York) revival of Charles Weidman's "Candide," originally presented in 1933.

graphical solo cycle, "On My Mother's Side," and his more recent portrait of Abraham Lincoln in "A House Divided—". Most frequently, however, it is either gaily comic or devastatingly satirical, for he has a wonderful gift for observing and visualizing the vagaries of men and manners.

His little solo called "Kinetic Pantomime" is a study in pure nonsense, and the same general idea of comedy pantomime that actually means nothing in spite of seeming to, was developed in an excellent group work called "Opus 51." In the main, though, he stays closer to recognizable comment, ranging all the way from his amused biography of his father, "And Daddy Was a Fireman," to the hilarious kidding of the old silent movies, called "Flickers." Somewhere in between these two extremes are his choreographic versions of Voltaire's "Candide" and Max Beerbohm's "Happy Hypocrite."

In "A House Divided—" he strikes the most serious note of his career. If the idea of making a dancing figure of Lincoln seems incongruous, it proves in his sensitive hands to be instead altogether convincing and deeply intuitive.

He and Humphrey have danced very generally in each other's works from the start. He has created the choreography for a scene of his own in each of her group compositions, "Theatre Piece" and "New Dance," and by way of return, her performance of the Hollywood vampire in "Flickers" and the sordid wife in "This Passion" were among the happiest elements of those works in performance. In 1945, however, on the retirement of Humphrey, he formed a company of his own including, among others, such excellent young dancers as Nadine Gae, Saida Gerard and Peter Hamilton. With the Lincoln work, an amusingly archaic version of "David and Goliath," and several other numbers in the repertoire, he has started a new period of his career—for the first time, entirely on his own.

Charles Weidman as Abraham Lincoln in "A House Divided—" (1945).

The artist who has come to be most generally the symbol of the modern dance in the popular mind is that other rebel from Denishawn, Martha Graham. This is easy to understand, for though the casual public might not immediately recognize the true quality of her art, it could not fail to note that her independent approach to the dance resulted in the same kind of startling surface qualities as had already been found in modern painting and modern music. It was inevitable, then, that her dancing should be called "ugly," "angular," "obscure" and—"modern." Since she was of challenging personality, she created a sharp division of opinion, some of it violently antagonistic, some just as vigorously sympathetic, and all of it transforming her into a kind of one-woman "cause célèbre." With the passage of the years, the sharpness of this cleavage has been tempered, and she has won a wide audience, not only because she has softened somewhat with maturity as an artist but also because with increasing familiarity her work has ceased to appear strange and perverse, which, as a matter of fact, it never was. It remains, nevertheless, always provocative, even in its least experimental manifestations.

Interestingly enough, in view of the once so frequent accusations that she was too abstract, in her Denishawn days Graham was considered too theatrical to be admitted to the concert company. Instead she appeared chiefly in the vaudeville branch of the organization's activity, including especially the Aztec dance-drama, "Xochitl," with Ted Shawn. When she left Denishawn in 1923 it was to appear in the "Greenwich Village Follies," and even when she turned independently to the recital field, she still danced Hindu and Greek and exotic dances with many of the typical Denishawn trappings, and was described as "graceful," "pictorial" and without much technique.

Martha Graham in "Salem Shore" (1943).

This, however, was exactly the approach against which she was in the process of rebelling, and when she had ultimately found her own style, it was in every respect the direct opposite of this. The adjectives that were now applied to her were "stark" and "gymnastic," for she had stripped away everything but the essentials, not only of stage paraphernalia but of movement itself. In revolt against the arbitrary softness of the old sentimental style of legato movements, she evolved what she called percussive movement; that is, movement initiated by a sharp attack like that of a drum beat. Instead of producing diffuse gestures that seemed to float off indefinitely into space, she sought to center the body and to integrate its movement within its own sphere of action.

Her entire approach to the dance, indeed, in creative method as well as in technique, has been one of integration, as if she were trying to focus the world around her, or at least those aspects of it that immediately inspired her, within herself in order to communicate it in its highly concentrated essence. Her purpose is to evoke a heightened awareness of life, not merely to present its surface. To this she is stimulated by multifarious and unpredictable objects; her environment, both mental and physical, is a continual source of creative inspiration, and her artistic life is constantly being shaped and re-shaped, colored and recolored, by its sensitivity to its surroundings. Sometimes it is large and heroic influences that touch her into creation—the vast American landscape, the cultural attitude of the American Indian, the ritual practices of antiquity, the ugliness of provincial intolerance; sometimes

Martha Graham and group in "Act of Judgment" (1934).

it is comparatively small and specific phenomena—maps, the flower paintings of Georgia O'Keeffe, the poems of Emily Dickinson, the warped world of the Brontës.

If the forms and surfaces of the works thus inspired are necessarily vastly different, there remains beneath them, nevertheless, a constant element which is the personal style of the artist herslf—a passionate intensity that is so controlled as to become a kind of incandescent quietness, with an immersion in the emotional elements of a situation which brings movement of curious form and unique eloquence virtually out of the subconscious.

It is useless to look for objective theory in a style so completely personal, so completely outside the realm of the intellectual. It has little continuity with the past, little projection into the future; it exists solely in the perfection of its own being here and now. Graham has raised the level of the art immeasurably and has become one of the most potent influences in the entire world of the dance, yet she has done so without establishing any systems, any generalities of procedure, that are applicable to the art as a whole or to its continuity of development. Her greatness is in an almost unique sense her own.

Throughout her career she has been endlessly experimental, not only in matters of purely choreographic concern but also in the evolving of a style of production. In costuming she was early a radical in her use of both materials and designs. Her approach to stage setting has capitalized the very

Martha Graham and group in "Primitive Mysteries," orignally produced in 1931.

Scene from Graham's "Appalachian Spring" (1944). Erick Hawkins in foreground. Opposite page: Martha Graham and May O'Donnell in "Herodiade" (1944).

financial stringencies of the dance world which would seem to have limited it, and has developed a remarkably effective use of isolated bits of décor, sculpturesque "objects" and properties instead of more conventional scenery. Her employment of words, which dates way back to the "Sarabande" and "Pantomime" of the suite called "Transitions" in 1934, has been consistently well-motivated and fitted into the particular frame of the work at issue. Her musical experimentation has been less plastic and in general less happy, but she has had some fine scores by Aaron Copland, Paul Hindemith. Louis Horst (her longtime musical director, critic and mentor), Lehman Engel, Wallingford Riegger, Robert McBride and Paul Nordoff.

At present she has emerged into a rich period of theatre pieces—"Letter to the World," "Deaths and Entrances," "Appalachian Spring," "Herodiade," "Dark Meadow," "Punch and the Judy," "Every Soul Is a Circus," and the solo, "Salem Shore," which is substantially as much of a drama as any of them—all composed since 1939. But the earlier years teem with works of equal artistic significance, if generally of smaller dimensions. "Adolescence," "Heretic," "Primitive Mysteries," Dithyrambic," "Lamentation," "Primitive Canticles," "Ekstasis," "Frenetic Rhythms," "Sarabande," "Act of Piety," "Frontier," "El Penitente," are all of considerably more than passing moment, though many of them are now forgotten even by Graham herself.

It is assuredly worthy of note that this artist, once set apart from all her colleagues as the most "difficult" and "obscure" practitioner of an art generally pronounced "arty," has become today, without the slightest compromise, what is known as "good box-office," and set a record by playing a full season of two weeks on Broadway.

134

HELEN TAMIRIS

Helen Tamiris, one of the most important of the pioneers of this important second generation, hails from a background quite apart from that of her three colleagues who came from Denishawn. Her first training was in the classes of Irene Lewisohn, who was later to make a major contribution to the American dance as director of the Neighborhood Playhouse with its school and producing center. The Metropolitan Opera ballet school, a touring Italian opera company ballet in South America, the class of Michel Fokine (all of which she heartily disliked), a brief sampling of the Duncan school, which pleased her no better, led her to the conviction that the kind of dancing she wanted to do would have to be of her own making. Night clubs, revues and movie-house presentations supported her while she worked it out.

She had come from an artistic family, with two painters for brothers, and she was very much in touch with the creative movements of the day in all the arts. It is not surprising, then, to find her early recitals, when she got around to the point in 1927 where she was ready to give them, sponsored by J. B. Neumann and the New Art Circle. It is not surprising, either, that the music she danced to was by Poulenc, Satie and Florent Schmitt; John Powell, Louis Gruenberg and George Gershwin. This seems commonplace enough, perhaps, until we remember that the most popular dance composers of the day were still Brahms and Schubert and Chopin and Mendelssohn, with a touch of Scriabin and Debussy for spice.

These first programs were listed as "Dance Moods" and were divided into "Moods Diverse" and "American Moods". They were extremely experimental dances in many ways; one of them was danced without accompaniment, another used as music the patterned beating of piano strings, still another used a siren, several of them made conscious use of movements adapted from athletics, the Gershwin was jazz treated seriously, two of them were Negro spirituals, one of them experimented briefly with nudity. All of them were characterized by direct and vigorous movement of great inherent beauty, backed by a lively and completely contemporaneous mind.

Helen Tamiris in "Negro Spirituals" (1929).

Opposite page: Scene from Tamiris's "How Long Brethren?", presented by the Federal Theatre, New York (1937).

Since Tamiris has always been a clear thinker and supremely articulate, it is characteristic that her basic theory was printed as a "Manifest" in one of her early programs. This is not only an interesting historical document, indicative of the insurgency in the dance world in that stimulating day, but also a key to Tamiris's individual practice, which though it has been enriched as she has progressed, is substantially outlined here. It reads as follows:

Art is international, but the artist is a product of nationality and his principal duty to himself is to express the spirit of his race.

* * *

A new civilization always creates new forms in art.

* * *

We must not forget the age we live in.

* * *

There are no general rules. Each original work of art creates its own code.

* * *

The aim of the dance is not to narrate (anecdotes, stories, fables, legends, etc.), by means of mimic tricks and other established choreographical forms. Dancing is simply movement with a personal conception of rhythm.

* * *

Costumes and music are complements of the dance. A dancer's creation should stand the test in the nude and the experience of motion without music.

* * *

Sincerity is based on simplicity. A sincere approach to art is always done through simple forms.

* * *

Authenticity tries to convince with the exact reproduction of details: costumes, postures, regional music and photographic make-up. A dancer must create his own reality, independent of the reality we live in. Reality has no interest for what it actually is but for what the artist sees in it.

* * *

Toe dancing. . . . Why not dance on the palms of the hands?

* * *

To give primary importance to facial expression is just as bad as to give primary importance to the feet. Both are elements of the ensemble, spokes of the same wheel—neither is the center.

* * *

It is false to create atmosphere or mood with exact reproduction of costumes belonging to a period or contemporary with a character. It makes one think of children who, to appear as men, paste moustaches on their faces.

* * *

The word pattern has become a standard term for choreography, decorative poses and external attitudes. Pattern is really what style is in any other art: an individual form of expression.

* * *

The dance of today is plagued with exotic gestures, mannerisms and ideas borrowed from literature, philosophy, sculpture and painting. Will people never rebel against artificialities, pseudo-romanticism and affected sophistication? The dance of today must have a dynamic tempo and be vital, precise, spontaneous, free, normal, natural and human.

* * *

Tamiris has never lost her interest in experimentation. For several seasons, for example, she worked on the idea of self-accompaniment, using cymbals, triangles, wood-blocks, gourd rattles and the like. Even outside of purely artistic matters she has been steadily adventurous; it was she who organized the Dance Repertory Theatre, in which for the first time, all four of the modern dancers of this lively second generation pooled their interests in seasons of joint performances in 1930 and 1931. In the days of the Federal Theatre Project, she was the most active spirit in its department of dance production in New York.

For this organization she produced one of her most interesting group works, "How Long, Brethren?" set to Negro songs of protest. Later she made excellent use of other groups of songs as background material. "Liberty Song" employed songs of the American Revolution, and a charming suite of "Bayou Ballads" was set to songs from Louisiana.

Tamiris's sound instinct for the theatre has led her of recent seasons into the staging of dances for Broadway musical productions, in which she has been conspicuously successful, sacrificing nothing of her integrity as an artist but managing at the same time to capture the essential flavor and style of both the musical theatre as a whole and the individual production in particular. Her resounding successes have included "Up in Central Park," "Annie, Get Your Gun," and the revival of "Show Boat." In this last she has used Negro concert dancers, including the brilliant young Pearl Primus, with especially gratifying results.

Left: Helen Tamiris in "Liberty Song" (1942). Center: Helen Tamiris. Right: Daniel Nagrin and Helen Tamiris in "Bayou Ballads" (1944).

THIRD GENERATION

It is clear that with dance activities resuming on something of a more normal basis now that World War II has ended, the third generation of the modern dance must be reckoned with as a definite force. It is too early as yet to hazard any guesses as to the directions which its new radicalisms will take when they finally develop, as they necessarily must do, but the field is manifestly rich with young artists of ability.

There are, for example, two new groups with conspicuous accomplishments to their credit, one of them consisting of Jane Dudley, Sophie Maslow and William Bales, and the other headed by José Limon and Beatrice Seckler, all of them products of the schools and companies of Graham, Humphrey, Weidman and Holm. The Dudley-Maslow-Bales Trio was formed in 1942, and in its debut performance presented a group work composed by Maslow which took its place at once as a little masterpiece. It is called "Folksay" and employs spoken passages from Carl Sandburg's "The People Yes," together with folk songs, as its background. The trio has also produced a number of smaller pieces of interest by all three choreographers and has danced them all excellently.

The other group was formed upon Limon's release from military service in 1945, with him as its moving spirit but with Doris Humphrey as general director. Its repertoire consists chiefly of his compositions, but Humphrey herself has created two works for it. As a dancer Limon is generally conceded to be the leading male artist of his generation, and Seckler is among the most gifted dancers in the field, capable in both drama and comedy, unique in personal style and, like Limon, with an en-

Left: Dorothy Bird, José Limon and Beatrice Seckler in "Concerto." Right: Esther Junger.

Pauline Koner.　　　　　　　　　　　　Eleanor King.

Below left: José Limon in "Danzas Mexicanas." Right: Beatrice Seckler in "Eden Tree."

Jane Dudley in "Short Story."

Left to right: Valerie Bettis in "The Desperate Heart." William Bales in "Adios." Jean Erdman in "Dawn Song." Merce Cunningham and Jean Erdman in "Credo in Us."

dowment of superlative movement. Dorothy Bird, another delightful artist, was originally the third member of the group, but withdrew at the end of the first season for other activities.

Valerie Bettis, who came out of Hanya Holm's company, has an outstanding talent for movement and an exciting stage presence. She has made interesting use of unorthodox music and of speech, and her solo dance, "The Desperate Heart," for which John Brinnin wrote a background poem, is a work of the first rank. That she is one of the most vital forces in the new generation is unmistakable.

Sybil Shearer, a former member of the Humphrey-Weidman company, who makes her headquarters in Chicago, is another artist of extraordinary power and originality. She has not only an astounding technique but also a creative approach unlike that of any other artist in the field. Her work is curiously eloquent, her movement created by the sheerest intuition, and her concepts altogether off the beaten track. Though her approach is highly neurotic and sometimes headstrong, it is thoroughly honest and uncompromising, and her effect on the field can scarcely fail to be of considerable moment.

Eleanor King, also a Humphrey-Weidman alumna, has grasped clearly that basic relation between inner meaning and actual movement which is the essence of the modern dance. This she has put into form in several excellent solo suites such as "Roads to Hell" and "Characters of the Annunciation," and in two extraordinarily evocative dances to bits of Schoenberg's "Pierrot Lunaire" and to music of Alban Berg. These last two deal in substrata of the mind that are rarely touched in the dance, but are haunting and strangely disturbing. In her present headquarters in Seattle she is working toward the creation of a dance group of her own, for ensemble composition has interested her since her early composition of the choric drama, "Icaro."

Jean Erdman, a former member of Martha Graham's company, is evolving an interesting and thoroughly individual style of composition that is strongly influenced by current trends in modern poetry, painting and music. She utilizes with great imagination experiments in music and speech as well as in movement itself. Though she is a very young artist, still struggling in a degree against an intellectual approach, her talent is clearly established in such compositions as the trio called "Daughters of the Lonesome Isle," and such contrasting solos as "Flight" and "Creature on a Journey."

Iris Mabry is another young artist of unquestionable gifts. She is just emerging into the field, but already she has exhibited a personal style of great individuality, an extraordinary quality of movement and a rich invention.

Sophie Maslow in "Folksay."

A development that is destined to have great significance in the postwar dance world is the emergence of a number of highly gifted Negro artists. As a direct result of the old minstrel tradition, the Negro has heretofore been confined almost exclusively to the inertias of the entertainment field, but with the advent of the modern dance, in which he has found a medium for expressing himself in forms of his own devising, he has begun to find his rightful place in the creative arts and to do so with impressive results.

There has been fine and courageous leadership in this important field of American art; Catherine Dunham, the late Hemsley Winfield, the Creative Dance Group of Hampton Institute, the New Dance Group with its breaking down of the color line, all take high places in the list. From Africa has come Asadata Dafora with the traditions of the mother country, and from the Caribbean, Belle Rosette and Josephine Prémice have brought another significant cultural tradition. Eventually, no doubt, the purely objective racial approach to the art will give place to a more universal attitude in which the artist dances simply as an individual human being, allowing his racial heritage to voice itself freely through him but not to limit his range of subject and content.

It is from the leadership of such artists as Dunham and Pearl Primus that this broadening of base seems likely to be achieved, for though both of them are scholarly young women who have studied the African and Caribbean as well as the early American backgrounds of the Negro dance, they are primarily artists, sensitive to their immediate environment and ready to translate it into contemporary art. Dunham has won wide success in recent seasons in the theatrical and motion picture fields, but she has also retained her interest in the more serious aspects of the dance and its ideals, has established a school of broad scope and is a potent influence in the field. Primus has exhibited magnificent gifts in the concert dance. Her technical powers are prodigious, she has temperament, imagination and a high artistic integrity which place her at once among the best young dancers of the day, regardless of race.

Left: Katherine Dunham in her "Tropical Revue."

Right: Belle Rosette.

Pearl Primus.

The total outlook for the future, then, is distinctly bright throughout the entire dance field. Against a background of two generations of dauntless and aggressive pioneering and of solid accomplishment, the new generation shows every sign of eagerness and ability to carry on toward ever fuller realizations of the same high purposes.

Josephine Prémice.

PART FIVE

Dance in the Technological Era

I T GOES without saying, perhaps, that so sensitive a medium as the dance will sooner or later be affected as strongly by the scientific and mechanical progress of today as it has been in the past by social, political and philosophical changes in its environment. Already there are visible certain results in the fields of sound recording, moving pictures and television, and though the accomplishment has not yet been very great in any of them, at least directions of future progress are indicated.

The enormous improvement in the recording of music, and also in the equipment by which the recordings can be played back with amplification suitable for large halls, has made it possible for dancers to dance to music played on all sorts of instruments that are not to be found in the conventional orchestra. Such a dancer as La Meri, for example, who has collected ethnological dances from many remote sections of the world, can now present them with authentic music actually recorded by native musicians with native instruments, whereas it would be manifestly impossible to carry around with her separate orchestras of native musicians from India, Java, Japan, the Philippines, Hawaii, Spain.

Quite apart from these exotic instances, recorded music makes possible many modern experiments. When Hanya Holm presented "Trend" in New York in 1937, one of her most interesting innovations was her use of a recorded score, which employed not only the music written for small orchestra by Wallingford Riegger, but also the "Ionization" of Edgar Varèse, which is scored exclusively for percussion and demands instruments altogether outside the orthodox orchestra, and Varèse's "Octandre" for woodwinds. Most of this music was specially recorded, and equipment for its reproduction in performance was devised by Mirko Paneyko. The result was an extraordinary and a revolutionary use of mechanical means for the creation of a virtually new type of music. The venture proved prohibitively expensive, but at least it disclosed the latent potentialities of mechanical music.

Television is likely to have little effect upon the changing forms of the dance, but the greatest possible effect upon the popularization of them. Essentially the televised form of a dance is exactly the same as the stage form, and this will ultimately permit millions of people in remote districts to see

Marc Platt in his "Hitler" dance in Columbia's "Tonight and Every Night."

Gene Kelly and Jerry, the Mouse, in the M-G-M film, "Anchors Aweigh."

great works of art which could not be toured in personal performance over so wide an area in many years of constant traveling by the artists performing them.

The field of television is so young, however, that it is dangerous to prophesy what it may or may not be able eventually to do. It has already come a long way from those early broadcasts by the Columbia Broadcasting System back in 1931 when Tashamira, the charming dancer from Croatia, undertook to pioneer in the development of television compositions. Then the medium was so primitive that not even the whole body of the dancer could be projected, the space within which she could move was approximately six feet square, and the image of her carefully designed movements of torso, arms and head emerged on the screen dimly in red with a mesh of black lines over it. All that is past and gone, of course, and now whole companies of dancers move on comparatively spacious stages and the reception is clear. No doubt when it becomes practicable to manufacture receiving sets in quantity, dancing will play an increasingly large part in the available programs that are broadcast.

THE FIELD OF THE MOTION PICTURE

It is the motion picture, however, that would seem to offer the greatest new field for the dance, evolving ultimately a type of dance that is as different from the stage dance as the screen play is from the stage play. Surprisingly enough, very little of consequence has been done in this medium in spite of the miles of celluloid that have been devoted to dancing.

When the motion picture camera was new, nothing could have been more obvious as a subject to exploit its possibilities than a dancing figure. In a catalogue of dance films compiled by George Amberg, curator of the dance and theatre collection of the Museum of Modern Art in New York, and published in the May 1945 issue of Dance Index, there are listed any number of items made as early as 1897 by Edison and International Photographic Films. Their average length was fifty feet and their titles include such things as "Fantastic Toe Dance," "Bowery Waltz," "Skirt Dance," "Coquette Dance," "Dance of Rejoicing" by Fiji Islanders. That is roughly fifty years ago and cameras have been trained on dancers of one sort or another pretty steadily ever since, but the dance has still not received the treatment of which it is capable.

Actually the camera has two quite different functions in this connection: it can be either a mechanism for simply recording a dance exactly as it is performed on the stage, or it can be an instrument of art working in collaboration with a dance designer to create a purely cinematic dance that could not possibly be done on the stage. The former function is a highly important one and can be turned advantageously to the recording and preserving of great performances of great works, just as the phonograph records and preserves great musical performances.

But this has little to do with the art of the screen; that depends entirely upon the second function of the camera. Here is involved the use of dissolves and angle shots and close-ups and double exposure and slow motion and all the varied visual miracles that only motion photography can achieve. But

Archie Savage and Katherine Dunham in Warner Brothers' "Carnival of "Rhythm."

Scene from Warner Brothers' film of Massine's "Capriccio Espagnol," danced by the Ballet Russe de Monte Carlo, and entitled "Spanish Fiesta" on the screen.

Scene from Sophie Maslow's "Folksay," danced by the New Dance Group, as it was televised by the Columbia Broadcasting System.

obviously a dance that is to be so photographed must be designed for such treatment. To chop up and piece together a stage dance along these cinematic lines is to destroy its effectiveness as a stage dance and to give it no compensatory value as a film. The result is approximately parallel to what would happen if a sound engineer attempted the phonograph recording of a symphony by jumping from a passage in the first movement to a comparable passage in the last movement and back again, by blotting out the sound of all the instruments except the violins when they happen to be playing an ingratiating melody, etc. The distortion is just as great in one case as in the other. Yet dances are generally treated in just this way in the majority of the films in which they occur; now we see a whole line of dancers, now the camera moves up to one central figure, now to the face alone and again down to the feet; then we jump suddenly to a position overhead and catch a fleeting glimpse of the whole group from above, and so forth. No form, no composition, no design, can possibly emerge, and the dance is accordingly rendered ineffective.

FRED ASTAIRE

The solution to the problem is not an easy one, but several noteworthy attacks have been made upon it. Fred Astaire, for example, throughout his long and brilliant screen career has consistently opposed all camera tricks that would interfere with his dances. This may not be progressive cinema practice but it has served to protect the dancing of one of the greatest of American dancers. Astaire has an admirable sense of form and a genius for rhythm, both of which would be totally destroyed on the screen by the juggling of dance phrases for the sake of camera effects. Whatever his dances may lack as cinema art, at least they have used the camera well as a recording medium.

In "Yolanda and the Thief," however, he has also participated in some more experimental practices which still do not conflict with his customary attitude to the camera. Here, as a hard-boiled confidence man in a lusciously technicolored mythical Latin-American country, he is the leading figure in a dream ballet which is perhaps as beautiful a dance number as the screen has yet achieved. Instead of consisting of a formal routine more or less in one spot, it involves traveling choreographically through a number of scenes and makes a conscious use of space as it cannot very well be used except in the films. The choreographer in this case was Eugene Loring, the director was Vincente Minelli, who has proven his taste and visual imagination on more than one occassion; the excellent settings were by Edwin Willis, and the music was by Arthur Freed, who was also the producer. From such a collaboration as this many hopeful developments can be expected.

This element of space is one thing in which the stage can never compete with the screen. The latter can achieve virtually limitless vistas and perspectives, can work on stages of enormous dimensions if it chooses, and by change of focus and distance from the camera can alter at will the relation between the dancing figures and their space environment.

To be sure, other films besides "Yolanda" have recognized these possibilities. To mention two which did so effectively, there are "Cover Girl" and "Tonight and Every Night," for which Jack Cole and Val Raset are credited with the choreography. Mr. Cole, a former Denishawn boy who brings

Lucille Bremer and Fred Astaire in the dream ballet from the Metro-Goldwyn-Mayer film, "Yolanda and the Thief."

a fine artistic background to his work as a dance director, should be especially watched for what he may be able to accomplish in these new technological fields.

In this latter film, incidentally, Marc Platt, young American dancer, formerly of the Ballet Russe de Monte Carlo and later in the original production of "Oklahoma," made his screen debut in an excellent and unusual number in which he danced what was supposed in the story to be an improvisation to a speech by Hitler and other miscellaneous items that happened to be coming in on the radio.

GENE KELLY

An approach all his own is that of Gene Kelly, who may very well be the most important figure on the Hollywood dance scene at the moment. Not only has he a lively imagination as a dancer and a creator of dances, but he is also keenly aware of the camera's unique possibilities, which most dancers are not. He is, therefore, at the opposite extreme from Astaire. In "Cover Girl" and "Anchors Aweigh" he has produced, among a number of first-rate pieces, two notable ones which

153

Gene Kelly in his "Alter Ego" dance in Columbia's film, "Cover Girl."

could not conceivably have been done in any medium but that of the screen. In the former, by the use of double exposure and phenomenal timing, he does a superb dance in which he has an emotional struggle with his alter ego. In the latter, he dances with M-G-M's cartoon figure of Jerry, the Mouse —himself in his normal dimensions and the mouse as an animated line drawing. Both of these, aside from their effectiveness in their own right, are adventuresome technical exploits which show clearly Kelly's awareness of the camera's range and adaptability. Nobody else in Hollywood has come so near to the pure medium of cinema dance, and since what he does is not in the least arty, in spite of the fact that it is deliberate aesthetic pioneering, there would seem to be no limit to the extent of his future experimentation along the same lines, and with the wholehearted support of the box-office. This is a heartening and significant phenomenon.

It is a curious fact that the most important screen dancers are all men. By some inexplicable process, most of the feminine dancers who make a success in Hollywood are transformed sooner or later into dramatic stars. This was true even of Pavlova, whose only film, back in 1916, was "The Dumb Girl of Portici" in which she played a straight dramatic role. This is perhaps to be explained by the non-existence at that time of any sound film by means of which her dancing could have its normal

Rita Hayworth dancing down an enormous ramp in Columbia's "Cover Girl."

musical accompaniment. But much the same thing has happened to Ginger Rogers, Rita Hayworth, Tamara Toumanova, Viola Essen, even though the sound film is now the conventional medium.

The development of sound, as a matter of fact, served to give the element of rhythm its proper audible support and thus to make dance films possible. But the dance is a space art just as much as it is an art of rhythm, and not until the screen has perfected the three-dimensional film will it become fully a medium for dancing. This next technological step forward will make feasible for the first time a truly accurate recording of stage dances, and will also open up a broad new field for experimentation with purely cinematic dance forms.

INDEX

PICTURE CREDITS